DAVID SERPA
ZEN BUSINESS

AN EASTERN APPROACH TO THE WESTERN BUSINESS CLIMATE.

FOREWORD BY NICK BALDWIN

"A MUST READ!"
-David Godwin, LtCol (Ret), USMC AnnieMac Home Mortgage

"DAVID SERPA CAPTURES THE VERY ESSENCE OF TRUTH IN ZEN BUSINESS."
-Susan Ebert, Broker/Owner, Signature Real Estate Group.

"LOVE, LOVE, LOVE THIS BOOK. IT'S ABSOLUTELY THE BEST BOOK TO TAKE WITH YOU INTO THIS NEW DECADE!"
-Rosie Rodriguez, Best-Selling Author, Inspiring Thought Leader, & Speaker.

"HIGHLY RECOMMENDED!"
-Borino, Real Estate Coach, Author of the EXPIRED PLUS and FSBORINO.

"THIS BOOK WILL MAKE A DIFFERENCE."
-Rick Geha, Motivational Speaker, Life Coach, Freedom Pathfinder.

DAVID SERPA

David Serpa is a writer, a musician, and an agent/owner with eXp realty. He is a veteran of the United States Marine Corps and lives in Southern California with his blended family of seven.

Zen Business

An Eastern approach to the Western Business Climate.

By David Serpa

Dedication

This book is dedicated to my wife, Katie Serpa, my spiritual partner in business and in life. Thank you for your insight, your perspective, and your gentle guidance.

Table of Contents

- I. Praise for Zen Business................................ 6
- II. Foreword by Nick Baldwin......................... 10
- III. Introduction to Zen Business..................... 13
1. Bodhicitta: Altruistic Service........................... 22
2. Now.. 35
3. Zazen & Mushin: Meditation & No Mind.............. 50
4. Detachment... 61
5. Bushido: The Samurai Code............................ 81
6. Play... 92
7. Stress... 103
8. Principles of Zen Business........................... 118
    - Efficiency... 118
    - Presence... 122
    - Present Goals..................................... 124
    - Self-Reflection................................... 125
    - Awareness.. 125
    - Breath Control.................................... 126
    - Purposelessness................................. 128
    - Enough... 129
9. Die Before You Die....................................... 131
10. Nirvana & Bodhi.. 159

I.   Praise for Zen Business

*

"ZEN BUSINESS is a breath of fresh air in the crowded (and often stuffy) world of business coaching. David Serpa molds an old Eastern wisdom into practical advice that will guide you through the ups and downs of business. You will discover that there is more to success than just HUSTLE! Yes, you can be a Rockstar agent while still having a life filled with joy, balance, and peace of mind. Highly recommended!"

Borino, Real Estate Coach, Author of the EXPIRED PLUS and FSBORINO.

*

"'When we remember we enjoy giving it is easier to give without the expectation.' 'Be curious about life, perpetually interested, willing to be influenced, and always open to being wrong.' David Serpa captures the very essence of truth in ZEN BUSINESS. Tears joyfully flooded my face drenching my heart with the water of life after reading this book. It is a

delightful journey of life, love, acceptance and unconditional truth of a heart searching and finding peace. I'm extremely thankful you have shared this work so the world may know true love. I love you David SERPA."

Susan Ebert, Broker/Owner, Signature Real Estate Group.

*

"I am so humbled and honored to know David Serpa. When we were in the Marine Corps, he continually amazed me with his breadth of knowledge on life and what it means to be happy. During my transition from the Marine Corps, I was very stressed out, until I read Zen Business. David continues to be a beacon of inspiration for me. He is a warrior and a hero. This book has opened my eyes to focus on the important things in life, like family and friends, which will fuel my success in business. A must read!"

David Godwin, LtCol (Ret), USMC AnnieMac Home Mortgage

*

"David has captured what most authors skip. He has used his personal experiences to get to the truth about succeeding in business. It's very rare that someone so young has leaned so much and, even more, has been successful in communicating it . I love his writings and his way of thinking. This book WILL make a difference."

Rick Geha, Motivational Speaker, Life Coach, Freedom Pathfinder.

*

"David Serpa hits the nail right on the head with his book, Zen Business. This book clearly defines what Zen is in business and exactly how one would achieve this Zen. This book is for everyone that thinks they don't need it, or don't know what it is, AND everyone that does know what it is and just can't figure out how to create it. Zen wasn't exactly what I thought it was and I think it will vary for every reader, but this book fits no matter what. Bravo Zulu David Serpa!

Tobie Love, Originating Branch Manager, CrossCountry Mortgage

"Love, love, love this book. It's absolutely the best book to take with you into this new decade! This is not another self-help book about life, or 10 steps to business. It is so much more profound! It speaks to your soul. David is one of the brightest minds and kindest souls on the planet. His ability to see through the superficial business environment of today's world, and help remind us of who we are as spiritual beings in service of others is incredible. I recommend this to any person who wants to find or fall in love with their purpose again! I honestly couldn't put it down."

Rosie Rodriguez, Best-Selling Author, Inspiring Thought Leader, & Speaker.

*

II.   Foreword by Nick Baldwin

When I first heard about David I asked him to speak at a conference I was hosting. We had talked on occasion through social media and email prior to the event, but to be honest, I didn't know much about him. However, by what I observed online, I was very intrigued.

When I first met David, it was in a crowd. He had long scraggly hair, a beard, large headphones around his neck (not plugged into anything on the other end) and a straw fedora; the textbook definition of "California Surfer" and he had the personality to match. David was relaxed yet lively and had this energy about him that was truly infectious. When he spoke on stage that week, the audience was captivated. But little did everyone know, behind that carefree and outgoing persona, he was suffering with some major inner turmoil. It was because of that inner struggle that David and I became close.

As someone who struggles with mental health issues and has a son with a neurological disorder, David and I bonded over our "superpower" brains. Mine is ADHD and his is autism. We confided in each other often about the rat race of the world and the obsessive, competitive nature of the real estate industry and how that affects us personally. How it's so easy to feel like you aren't enough, constantly wanting more, but also how quickly those desires can have a negative effect on your physical and emotional wellbeing. Enter the need for "Zen Business."

It was at my conference, Lab Coat Agents Live, that David introduced the world to "Zen Business." David has often been ahead of this conversation, and it's one that needs to be had. The constant competition in the business world can give someone the feeling of dissatisfaction in their life, comparing yourselves to the accomplishments of others and finding it difficult to be proud of your own is only becoming more prominent.

You'll find out in this book that David is a machine gunner, and his new outlook on life and business is quite the opposite of what you'd expect from someone who's been to places most will never understand (mentally and physically). His passion for putting service over a paycheck has made him the success he is today. Being transparent and vulnerable is not something you see too often, and it's people like David who are allowing others to embrace themselves and their lives where they currently are.

David once said to me, "There will always be someone who's doing more than you." As simple as that statement is, it's powerful. I know for a fact when David had this realization in his own life, his mindset shifted. We all must stop competing with others and start learning from them. Once we adopt a learning-based mind, we can truly be at peace with where we are headed because we begin to realize that our only competition is ourselves. This is one of the great lessons you'll take away from "Zen Business." Appreciating your life and accomplishments without the world saying you haven't done enough. We will get to where we want to be when we get there. No one is rushing you so go at your own pace and own it.

III.   Introduction to Zen Business

You could say Zen came into my life a few years ago after wrapping up *The Machine Gunner's Guide to Real Estate* but it would be more accurate to say these thoughts and feelings were always inside of me. I just didn't have the words and practices to turn them into a lifestyle and so I forgot myself.

At every corner and by most every person in the Western Business Climate I was encouraged to charge more, pay less, and systemize myself out of my business so I could concentrate on doing whatever I *want* to do. Many of my ideals were questioned, laughed at, or openly mocked by the "successful" and "unsuccessful" alike. While others took time to pause and reconsider or confess to me, in private side conversations, that they felt similarly about business.

The problem is that I enjoyed so much of what the west wanted to remove me from; service, camaraderie, squad objectives. I have no interest in spending my life riding jet skis or traveling for the sake of traveling. I have always had a servant's heart and volunteerism and integrity have been cornerstones of my business.

The idea of only doing what you are *the best in the world at* causes a great deal of anxiety when that was never an important ideal for me to begin with. That would assume that being the best was something I wanted.

I always enjoyed competition but camaraderie and teamwork were more important to me. I enjoyed the tribal atmosphere in the Marine Corps. I learned a lot about myself and the world through war and returning home from it. When I joined the Marine Corps, I joined to serve, not to be served.

However, I had interesting ideas of what service was, and was not, because I was not yet connected to the idea that we are all connected. I was still an *us against them* person. I only believed in *self-sacrifice* and didn't understand what it truly meant to *give*. I self-sacrificed a lot. I carried these principles with me into business.

This is not a book about real estate or my past. I want only to give some brief perspective on where I came from when I transitioned into real estate. As an industry outsider I had no idea people were keeping track of their sales numbers and that agents were ranked on an office, local, state and sometimes even a national level based on their production.

I made more money in my second month in real estate, than during any year in my life up unto this point, by being of service. I never thought about charging more, paying my administrative team less, or no longer working with people in lower price points. I just loved serving people and felt honored to serve again, and fortunate to have all this money coming in. After a while I even felt guilty. I wanted to teach others how to make a lot of money as well.

I won't tell my whole story here, that is for another book. The book that pushed me over the edge; *The Machine Gunner's Guide to Real Estate; Accuracy by*

Volume. It was pain, fear, and ego incarnate with moments where love is trying to shine through and make peace with the shattering world around me.

A lot of people have asked me *why the sudden infatuation with Zen?* The truth is; I could go Zen or I could go crazy. I tried crazy and it brought me back to Zen. I just enjoy my craziness more and accept myself for who I am. It does not make one sane to fit into a society that has lost its mind.

I was, and still am at times, an incessant over-thinker. The problem with always thinking is it is like *always talking to yourself*. Only crazy people do this. I did this for most of my life and for the last several years incessantly. Only giving myself brief moments of respite in the shower when *no mind* would allow me to take a break. Then suddenly I would be flooded with inspiration and reach for my phone, with wet hands, to write down some notes. Giving myself no peace. No space for me. No room for God, or The Oneness, to operate and come through. I was asleep, in many ways, drifting through my life as I was programmed to do.

I had so much I did not want to think about and so much I did not want to feel that my ego was in overdrive working to prevent that sort of pain again and because of this I predominately felt pain. I was carrying the pain along with the lessons I had learned with me into the future. I did not need to carry the pain. The lessons were already realized. The pain was unnecessary. I was only continuing to punish myself.

Much of the negative self-talk, I felt, pushed me to success. I was afraid of what would happen to my business and my successes if I stopped driving myself with a bullwhip. When you can't stand yourself silence is hard to handle. Your own company is unbearable and other people's problems are much more enticing to handle. After all, you can fix *their* problems, right?

Zen is not a religion. However, I believe it to be a spiritual practice. Ascension, or enlightenment, is not the untouchable thing we think it is, so far out in the future, on a hilltop, where we are much older and maybe a little skinnier, wearing spiritual clothing with a Shaman or a Priest sitting in a small room with incense burning. Nor is it being plummeted into an indoor swimming pool in front of a congregation of cheering and supportive people. Like happiness, it cannot be quested to or arrived at. We cannot rush enlightenment and take it by force, nor can we push it on others. We don't even have to put it off until we are older and wiser and done having fun.

While Zen is not a religion, it is a way of life which will help you see a moment in truth. Many people throughout the world use Zen Buddhism to better understand the mystical elements of their own religion. We will touch on many of these world religions in the final chapter while giving a little extra attention to Christianity, as the Religion of the West, as well as the life and teachings of Jesus, with the intention of showing you that *God* is much closer than you may think.

In this book we will dive into Zen principles and practices and see how we can apply these teachings to not only improve our businesses but our personal and spiritual lives as well. The people that say "balance is a lie" while switching between family, personal, church, and their professional lives are not realizing that all of these things are the same connected spiritual life practice. Nothing must fit into a compartment. No hats must be changed as you walk into your business, your church, or your home. We intuitively know these things to be true and yet we fight them so vigorously.

Zen gives us the ability to be free flowing as we live and die in each moment without expectations for those around us, ourselves, or with the intention of bending nature to our will. We can choose to act but let us do it with both eyes open. Is it best to achieve with dog-like focus or a general awareness?

I don't want to spend my time quantifying Zen, as this would defeat the purpose entirely, but instead give you an alternative way to look at business that might just make you feel a little better about your participation in it.

Zen Business is for the people that have hit the financial goals only to feel as empty as when they started, the people who have experienced business death and also those so afraid to start they do not move, which is death in and of itself. This book is for the perpetual seekers and the finders. The people looking beyond this realm and for the lessons to be learned from this one.

Death is not a bad thing. In business and in life. We are just terrified of it. When we live and die in every moment, we are ready when death comes knocking. We don't live a life in fear of death, which is a hell in and of itself. This book, I hope, will help you start truly living. Not for the future but for the moment.

I am not saying the Western approach of *more is more*, competition, delayed gratification, excess, and ego are bad. I want to offer an Eastern approach to the Western Business Lifestyle which has also consumed much of the East. The Western Business Lifestyle is easy to picture. Your mind is probably racing with thoughts of what it is now; the cars, the money, the houses, the sex, elaborate vacations, whatever. What does business look like when these things are not your aim? I am not telling you to forego pleasures of the flesh, just not to make these things the goal.

As someone who has identified with being a warrior, and is fond of different warrior cultures throughout the world, it is not my goal to make you into a pacifist nor am I encouraging you to be warful. Just be less consumed with everything you are not and you will find less of a necessity for war in your life as your ego will make room for other people.

As we study the Samurai and the Bushido, the way of the True Warrior, we find as much in the warrior culture about peace, taking steps to avoid war if possible, and in living life as we do about the actual *Art of War*. Having a deeper understanding of self, and warrior ethos, gives you the ability to act without depending on outside influences.

The first time I spoke on Zen Business was at LCA in 2018 and it was a side note to a larger speech I was delivering. It struck a chord with members of the audience and I was approached by a long line afterward. It resonated with people because it is a chord they hear within themselves. The thought that they are enough. They are whole and complete. This is a terrifying thought for some and immediately they are flooded with, *am I enough? Enough for what?* Others may say *of course I am enough! When have I ever not been enough?* While some are just ready to receive the message at this point in their lives and are overcome with emotion or a deep healing instantaneously. It is not a debate I am having with anyone. It is simply true; you are enough. *Phew!* You made it.

The rhythm of life is a much more natural thing than we give it credit for and we don't need to find balance, time-block, or constantly be worried about the future to be better in business today. No one ever became better by worrying about tomorrow.

I am grateful for the journey this book took me on and when it came into my life. It is the first book I have written that, in my opinion, is better than me. It is beyond my ability to deliver this book. I lean on quotes of people I would consider *fully-realized* or *ascended* to help strengthen this book.

Other times, as I wrote, I feel I could hardly take credit for the words that were coming from me. I was more of a vessel for higher consciousness, at my best, and an egoic pretender at my worst. It is up for you to decide. I probably spend a little time at both.

Global Awareness is better than it has ever been. We are coming into a Global Consciousness or an awakening. We are more connected than ever. We can no longer pretend that people do not exist on every level of our business. Every person is important and valuable. In every soul there is something to be treasured. Our job, if we should choose to think of ourselves as "leaders", is to provide the space for people to step into their own greatness. We cannot properly do this without first stepping into our own.

It is only through spreading awareness and using the tools at our disposal that we can help to spread global awakening or, at least, a good feeling. One community, one industry, one family, one individual at a time.

Real change starts internally. I don't claim to know where you are in your journey. I don't claim to be a master or an expert of any kind. For many of you, your experience with Zen starts now and I appreciate your readership and hope to do it justice. For others, I hope this will grant you a fresh perspective or deepen your understanding of your waters, or that you may forgive me for how shallow mine are at times. For some still, I hope to undo some of the damage I may have caused with my ego in my first book.

Now, I leave this in your hands to do with it what you will. I hope reading this book brings you as much peace as it brought me writing it. At the end, I hope you will be left with at least two takeaways which will give you peace throughout the rest your days; that you are whole and that *God* is much closer than you may think.

To separate life from business and business from life is to determine when it is appropriate to live! What is so different about *religion*, *work*, and *family life* that they must all be separated? In that may lie the problem.

I believe it all is a *spiritual practice* and I try to find myself *present* for it as often as possible. Where else is there to be other than right here, right now?

1. Bodhicitta: Altruistic Service

We have been taught to quest for happiness like it is a destination that can be traveled to or arrived at. We spend much of our days sacrificing today for tomorrow. Waiting for the day to come when the systems will be perfect, the right people will be in place, and we can start spending our time doing what we really want to do. But, what is it you really want to do?

The deeper problem is that most of us have no idea what we would really want to do with our extra time, or money, so when we get there it feels just as empty as when we got started. We are so fixated on this date on the calendar, the dream boards, and everything everyone else is doing and wanting that we often forget why we got started in the first place.

Attaining moderate entrepreneurial success is relatively easy in this country but we have few people worth modeling once we get there. The only people we have to look up to are often telling us "more" is the answer. I made a significant amount of money and there was no one around telling me "more isn't the answer."

Jim Carrey recently tweeted "I think everybody should get rich and famous and do everything they ever dreamed of so they can see that's not the answer." It's not that life is meaningless or worthless. It is that we are seeking our meaning in the wrong things.

We have been taught in our western business climate that *more things* equals *more happiness*. We have been taught to strive for stature and acclaim. We have believed that once we get there, we will be recognized, validated, and made whole.

We are a world asleep. We are a world divided. The more asleep we are the more division we crave. The more it will become "us" and "them". Some of us will be fortunate enough to be shaken violently from our slumbers.

When we are asleep stupid stuff seems important to us. We make the dream boards. We make financial goals. We set out to rectify the *life on the board* with the *life we are living* and we are taught to be discontented with our current possessions and stature. We are taught to be dissatisfied with where we are in life. We are constantly reminded of everyone that is doing better in every way, shape, and form.

We will continue to slumber until we are provided with an opportunity to wake up. Take the movie *Inception*. There is a group of people that are able to travel into another person's dreams to obtain information but in order to wake up they have to be jolted from their dream. They must fall.

Some of us are so deeply asleep in a dream within a dream, within a dream, that it will take multiple falls to wake us up. Others will spend an entire life willingly asleep, fighting to stay asleep, or even pretending to sleep. For this example look at Cypher in *The Matrix* enjoying his steak while talking to Agent Smith about being plugged back in and going to sleep. He says "I don't want to remember nothing. *Nothing.*

You understand? And, I want to be rich. Someone important, like an actor."

What is important and why? Looking past the words and into the actions is important when determining values in another person. A person could say one thing, and be acting another way entirely. The constant desires of people wanting to become someone and be somewhere they are not makes it so people rarely say what they mean. They are living in a dream world so they desire less reality.

Less reality requires more lies. In fact, it requires groupthink to takeover and the individual to be led astray by sleeping people promising things they do not have; riches, the perfect family, the perfect marriage. More often than naught the leaders of these types of businesses are falling apart at the seams. They may have the finances but could be leading an emotionally broken family. They may not even have the finances.

Illusion is an interesting animal. It takes a lot to keep up. We have all witnessed or been a part of relationships that are inauthentic. We all know people that you couldn't have a real conversation with if the house was burning down around both of you. They would rather sit in a burning room, remaining willfully ignorant until the end, than take the risk of leaving it. There are people that live their entire lives keeping the world at bay. The illusion in full swing.

My wife told me of a businessman making a video recently where he was teaching people how to feign authenticity in a business transaction. How extraordinarily counterintuitive! Wouldn't it be worthwhile considering actually being authentic? Seems like significantly less work to me.

If you have experienced an *Inception* level wake up in your life, there is a good chance you have found this book in your hand. Zen concepts and principles will rarely find their ways to the minds of someone not willing to hear them. They find people looking to wake up, not fighting to stay asleep.

Bodhicitta is the altruistic mind cherishing others over oneself. It is the purest way to be a part of a business, a family, a community, or even a country. It is pure service. Bodhicitta is naturally in you. It is what connects you to everything and makes you want to see other people do well. We have been taught to rebel against it. We have been taught in order for someone else to win, we must lose.

We have been told so many lies about business and life because we have been wired for consumerism. Buy more, be more, be better in all the artificial ways. We are consistently being sold *we are not enough* and we are buying. Not only are we enough, we are exactly what we need to be right now.

When we look at our economic relationships we have to question them. Is this person exercising service when working with me? Do they have my best interest in mind? The best business relationships are often when both companies, or individuals, have the best of the other person at the forefront of their consciousness.

More often than naught we are being told "you are not enough. You need me. Without me, you will fail. You need this money, you need these systems, you need my coaching, you need me." This is fear talking and selling fear itself.

What could possibly be wrong with you? We look to the sunset enthralled. We do not critique the stars. We marvel at nature and release judgement over it and, while we are made of all the same stuff, we critique ourselves in a way we never would any of these beautiful, natural occurrences. Are you not something to marvel over?

Why should I not exercise the same awe over every person I meet? When the mountains erupt from the plains below, scarring the valleys, erecting themselves against one another while reaching for the sky, setting bodies of water into motion, we do not look at these mountains and hold them accountable for the actions they have taken. Look at how everything has been shaped and love what stands before you. You are here.

There is this thought amongst many of us in the west; that a person is worth only as much as they can achieve. However, we don't feel that way about raw materials. We look at raw materials for their beauty now and for their potential later. Wood, oil, metal, granite all for what they can achieve when properly utilized. Human beings are our most under-utilized and under-valued resource on the planet. It is time we act like it.

I had a person write to me recently to inquire as to whether or not I am a genius. I don't say this to brag, I say this to further illustrate a point. It was a kind question to ask me, but I would argue that every person is/or has the capacity for genius. Our judgement of what is and is not genius is what has held us back.

Does it make a person a genius because they possess an ability that conveys properly in a test-taking atmosphere? I would argue we are overlooking genius if it must be placed somewhere to be studied. *Genius hands* caring for others may not have the words to express what they have learned or know innately to be true. An *emotional genius* may see much for which there are few words. Is it the ability to convey genius that makes one a genius, or is it the ability to receive, recognize, and properly help others utilize and craft their own? So much more could be done if we would just recognize our own abilities to serve humanity and worry less about what we call these occupations, or skills, or stop working to quantify our own level of expertise for the world. Who cares?

We have associated genius with accomplishment and recognition. We have required it to be quantifiable. You cannot take Einstein's brain apart to find genius, though it didn't stop them from trying. You will have to look much deeper. Dr. Viktor E. Frankl survived the concentration camps during World War II. He wrote in his book *Man's Search for Meaning*;

> *"But today's society is characterized by achievement orientation, and*

> *consequently it adores people who are successful and happy and, in particular, it adores the young. It virtually ignores the value of all those who are otherwise, and in so doing blurs the decisive difference between being valuable in the sense of dignity and being valuable in the sense of usefulness."*

What are the lessons we could hope to learn from the young? The reckless? We applaud these young, driving entrepreneurs as they speed forward sacrificing everything for the future. We expect their happiness to be associated with things. They expect it too. When it is not the falls begin to happen. The gentle pushes or the violent jolts into awakening.

We get addicted to the grind. We hustle for the sake of hustling. We work 24/7 and 365. We *sacrifice*. In learning to sacrifice for the superfluous we will be ever pushing towards a shifting goal in the distant future. We will find we are away from our families, away from ourselves, and feeling out of place and without purpose. The existential life crisis starts looming. Will it be a divorce? Will it be bankruptcy? What do we need to lose to learn we don't need to lose? Life is not some grand competition. Who am I competing with? Who do I need to beat?

We will dive more into comparative business, detachment, ego, and living in the present moment later, but this chapter is about something more important. This chapter is to let you know you were not wrong when you felt that first knee jerk reaction to someone telling you "you need more".

Getting a new car, a new house, a new job, a new wife, or doing more business is not the answer to your questions. You are enough right now. You are doing yourself a massive disservice by believing anything other than this and that is why *square one* in any new business venture is knowing you are enough.

Right now I am whole. Right now I am complete. Right now I need nothing. There is nothing that needs to be quested to, no grand journey, there is only right now. Jumping back to Dr. Viktor Frankl and *Man's Search for Meaning*;

> *"Life can be pulled by goals just as surely as it can be pushed by drives. Ever more people today have this means to live, but no meaning to live for. Happiness must happen, and the same holds for success; you have to let it happen by not caring about it." -Dr. Viktor E. Frankl*

By continuing to believe you are not enough, by continuing to believe you must sacrifice, by continuing to put off happiness for a date on the calendar somewhere in the future when you are better than you are now, you are denying yourself every moment between here and there. You may find you will never get to that date on the calendar. Will all of this have been for naught? Can we still enjoy the journey, while being aware of the destination? I would suggest this is the only way worth traveling.

Would awareness or complete focus be the best way to get a job done? I would have argued, and demonstrated at one point in my career, how complete and total focus and dedication was the only way to accomplish my goals. Now, I know that awareness is a much better option.

When focusing on the intention of a mission a military squad is aware of the mission, not primarily focused on the end goal. Crossing the street while being primarily focused on the end goal is great way to get yourself killed. When having sex focusing on the end goal denies you of every moment between initiation and finality. What a terrible way to live our lives! Yet this is what so many of us are doing.

We all see the entrepreneur working with dog like focus on their financial number or goal that will make them happy and satisfied. How desperately they sacrifice, slamming into everything, moving aimlessly forward. We may ask them why are you making these decisions? And they may respond that their coach, their broker, and everyone else is telling them this is what they should be doing. How well have their philosophies worked for them? Are they practicing what they preach?

Living your life while denying the present moment, living in full for the end, is like having sex for the climax. If there is no love involved, no connection to the moment or the person you are with, what are you doing? Are you making love to your life? Most of us are doing something much more vulgar with the lives we are living.

There is this great video my wife sent me by Jairek Robbins on the *Fearless Soul* Facebook Page. He tells the story about his friend, in real estate, who catches him sweeping the floors and tells him to stop. His friend suggests he should be paying someone else to do these things. His friend goes on;

> *"'Eventually you can grow it and scale it and become a business owner instead of a business operator, and at that point you have this 'four hour work week' where you check in a couple days a week and make sure everything's running perfectly and then you can finally sit back and enjoy your life.'*
>
> *"I said 'okay. But crazy question… If I can't enjoy sweeping the floor right now what makes you think I'm going to enjoy any of that?' I said 'Sounds cool.' I said 'on the other hand if I could learn how to fall in love with sweeping the floor right now I bet I could enjoy every step of that journey no matter where it takes me.' And*

> *there was this weird feeling of coming back to I am enough."*

  For those of us finding ourselves in various stages of enlightenment old principles will come around to challenge us in our way forward on this path. Some may find themselves very happy with the fast car, the fast life, the private planes, and the large homes. Others may find this existence seems egoic and empty and find an inner longing for something more. Bodhicitta is already in you finding its way to the surface. Stop fighting it. The altruistic mind cherishing others over oneself is a beautiful thing.

  How do we rectify cherishing others over oneself with business? We don't rectify it. They go hand in hand. When your primary focus is the service of others your business will naturally thrive as a biproduct. You will find your peace by finding your place.

> *"You can get everything in life you want if you will just help enough other people get what they want."*- Zig Ziglar

  The Dalai Lama explains Bodhicitta in a YouTube video entitled *H.H Dalai Lama's started crying while teaching Bodhicitta*. He explains;

> *"For the Lama it is fortunate to have this opportunity to teach about Bodhicitta. For you the disciples, also, this occasion for bodhicitta, the*

altruistic mind cherishing others over oneself..."

At this moment the Dalai Lama is overcome with emotion.

"Whoever generates this altruistic intention will find themselves setting out on the path to true happiness. We all want happiness and don't want suffering. Right?

"If you wish for real peace and harmony, there is nothing more one could ask for than reflecting on the bodhicitta. Usually, I do believe, and even say that, as recited in the Lama Choepa;

"'You are the Guru. The Personal Deity, the Angel, the Dharma Protector. As I do not seek any refuge other than you from now until my enlightenment please hook me with your compassion in this life, in the interim state, and throughout future lives. Relieve me from the fears of existence and peace, grant me all feats, befriend me forever, and avert all obstacles.'"

It is through acceptance and true connection to ourselves and one another that we can be present in and enjoy our journeys no matter what the outcome. Release the control of where you are headed while having a general idea of the direction and set out to be of service. Act and live now. There is no other way to live. Your life is happening whether you choose to enjoy it or not.

We are always serving. What are we serving? Who are we serving? These are questions worth analyzing if we should wish to live our lives enjoying a more permanent state of happiness not dependent on the whims of others, a destination, or the weather.

2. Now

I love Nike's slogan "just do it". Clean, concise, and to the point. However the more complete and finite slogan would be; "just do it, or don't". There's always that second option but it doesn't feel sexy to admit it and probably wouldn't sell as many shoes.

So often we act like there is one way to the top but there is not. The "top" is also extraordinarily subjective. Would you ever want to spend your life, a year, or even six months climbing to the top of someone else's mountain? Would you want to live someone else's story?

There is always the second option; don't do it. There is as much strength in saying "no" to a journey as there is in taking it, sometimes more. Too often we find ourselves weighing the *pros* and *cons* while driving ourselves mad. Going over and over each scenario in our head, following all of our potential choices to their natural conclusion.

We cannot wait for the perfect moment to act. We cannot wait for the stars to align before we decide to take decisive action forward. Being still is not the entire answer, being still is an answer.

Perfectionism, leads to procrastination, which leads to paralysis. Whether you are waiting for the perfect time to call your book of business, a tough client, or your grandma, waiting is not the decision.

If not now, when? Why not now? There are a million excuses and I will address many of them in this book but let's address one of my favorites head on; *the business plan.*

There is a great story recalled by a literary agent about how Jeff Bezos, the founder of Amazon, had pitched a room full of literary agents years ago and all of them had scoffed him off. "He doesn't even have a business plan" they laughed. Amazon now controls 60% of all book sales in the country and has started opening brick and mortar locations to compete with Barnes & Nobles.

Modern day business has fallen victim to the same bureaucratic and outdated mindsets as government. Working for the sake of working, not creating or using systems, and studying and analyzing vs. actually practicing.

There was a great chess master who once beat over 30 chess masters head-to-head simultaneously. When asked how he kept that many moves in his head he responded that he didn't. He only thought about the "next best move".

So often we know what the next best move is but we don't act or our busy schedule prevents us from acting. We over-schedule ourselves and push ourselves into business plans and then we are surprised when we continue to stay on the hamster wheel.

There is no time like the present. Furthermore, there is no time but the present. A business plan makes the assumption that the us on January 1st is going to know better than the us on June 1st. That the us on June 1st should somehow be accountable to the us on

January 1st. The less evolved, less enlightened person, operating with less knowledge than you have right now.

We know what we need to do. Why would we not do it? That's what we need to find out. Often there is a deep-seeded fear operating under the excuses holding us back from a more fully realized version of ourselves.

You can't help a person sell until you can help a person's soul. You may be able to temporarily provide them with fish but you will not teach them to fish for themselves on a permanent level. This keeps them dependent and further induces more fear.

When we are acting with Bodhicitta, the altruistic mind cherishing others over oneself, we want to see others thrive into their fullest potential. Business, as well as life, becomes a spiritual practice.

There is no separation between your spiritual and business life. No stopping and starting. No balance. Just a genuine flow back and forth between working spiritually in your business, with your family, and within yourself.

Martin Luther King Jr. acted in the presence full well knowing the grim outcome that could be waiting for him.

> *"Take the first step in faith. You don't have to see the whole staircase. Just the first step." -Martin Luther King Jr.*

You may not get to the top of that staircase but do you want to spend your whole life not knowing what's upstairs, who's up there, or if you're worth it? What happens if you don't take the shot?

> *"When you come to a fork in the road, take it." -Yogi Berra (attributed).*

We will explore attachment later in this book but attachment to time is a human experience. Establishing a business plan is giving the universe an opportunity to catch up with your external goals by deeming what amount of time is reasonable to pass before they can be accomplished. There is never anything but the present moment. If one cannot live there, one cannot live anywhere. Stop sacrificing your now for the future.

Why live our lives playing chess, seven moves ahead, when we must only concern ourselves with our next best move? Stop quantifying your goals in a way that makes other people comfortable. Everyone else sets goals in terms of *units* or a *dollar amount*. Let them.

If we concentrated more heavily on what is needed now vs. what we think will be needed in the future we will be free to act in the moment and will get significantly more done. Shoving aside the expectations, that blur with time, for the accomplishments which can be seen at the end of the day.

Isn't it interesting how big goals get when they are ten to fifteen years in the future? By applying the human constraints of time we are not allowing ourselves to think we could get there any sooner. These thoughts of the future are self-limiting. Instead, we should concentrate on feelings.

I am not telling you to suddenly cancel all your appointments and leave it up to the universe. I am telling you to stop holding yourself accountable to past versions of yourself. I am telling you to keep pieces of your day or week open to pursue inspired thought.

By being active, efficient, and aware we can avoid the hamster wheels of life. Doing work for the sake of doing work is what makes many of us feel useless. So many of us pretend to work, pretend to be with our families, and avoid our own minds at all cost.

We live guilt ridden lives constantly feeling terrible for all the things we are not doing even if we are actively participating in an activity that should be making our lives better. The real estate agent feeling guilty at the open house because it is a Saturday and they should be with their family. They don't commit to being present and having an effective open house. They don't make calls, they don't prospect. They feel bad. They go home to their family feeling lousy from an ineffective open house and they aren't present with their family. They check their phones, maybe sneak in a call or two. Perpetually feeling bad about existing in the present moment because they never do.

It is not easy to be present in this day and age. We no longer live in a time when people clock in and out, leaving the stress of the day at the office. Instead, we live blurring lines, trying to walk the tightrope of a "successful" business and a "successful" home life. Good. This forces us to get off the tightrope.

When you can always be reached, people always expect you to always be reachable. I keep my phone on *Do Not Disturb*. I can't stand the idea of wearing a *Jack in The Box* that could go off at any moment. For many of you, having the phone ring at any given time might not bother you. I used to answer my phone during just about anything. I would not let it go to voicemail.

I would answer my phone while at a listing appointment, if it's an active client, to see if it's an emergency. I would hang up the phone and explain to my prospective clients that I will do the same for them. Anytime. During dinner with my family. The middle of the night. It didn't matter. I would answer my phone. Neurotic people loved to work with me because I went around hearing everyone's neurosis.

There are very few reasons to answer the phone during dinner with your family. Most problems can wait 90 minutes. There are no reasons to answer the phone at 2am for a client. Nothing can be done in the business world at 2am. You have to begin to draw healthy boundaries at some point in your life or you will break.

When are you unreachable? When are you on fire for work? When are you on fire for your family? When do you find time for improvement? Draw healthy boundaries. Let people know when you will, and will not, pick up the phone when you meet with them, and reiterate this on your voicemail with an expectation of when they can expect a call back.

Saying to the world "Hi, you have reached David Serpa. If you have reached me after 6pm, please understand I am spending time with my family and your call will be returned the following morning. Thank you so much for understanding! I hope you have a great day!" It is then okay to call them back that evening if you have free time and feel inclined to do so. If you don't feel you can allow yourself an evening, or the systems aren't there yet, take two hours every evening to be unreachable to the world's problems. Give space for something more to reach you.

We are not working as much as we think we are and we are not playing as much as we should. We spend too much time keeping up the illusion of work and keeping up the illusion of relationships. Clocking in, and clocking out, putting in time, and going through the motions. We turn off our brains and turn off our hearts, and get to work. We can't be surprised when this undesirable habit follows us home.

We spend our time between sacrificing the now and numbing it out. What else could we hope for when we can't handle living in the present moment? The only way to combat this is with extreme presence and using your mind. If we don't use our mind, and work towards understanding it, we will continue to lose our days making someone else money, freeing up someone else's time, and continuing to lose our evenings to another Netflix episode starting in 5... 4... 3... 2... 1.

The world is designed in a way to help you lose faith, give you false faith, or pacify you in your goals. It will satisfy the settler with green pastures and a rushing river in exchange for his dreams of ever seeing a coastline. He will die with those dreams on his eyes, having never given way to wild intuition and a sense of adventure. Maybe he will even help several others in attaining their dreams but his feet will have never set far passed his river and into the sands of some far off coastline where all the water from his river is headed. His family will grow there, in those green pastures, and as he ages he will be full of reasons to never leave.

In the book *Outwitting The Devil* by Napoleon Hill he refers to this as *drifting*. Drifting is aimlessly going through life, being told what to do, and not thinking for yourself. Procrastinating on any dreams or thoughts of one's own. "The stalemate of all that is good." We drift through careers, relationships, marriages, parenting, and the next thing we know our lives have drifted right passed us. Napoleon Hill urges us to take control over our minds and awaken "the other self". He writes;

> *"My 'other self' has taught me to concentrate upon my purpose and to forget the plan by which it is to be attained when I go to prayer. I am not suggesting that material objects may be acquired without plans. What I am saying is that the power which translates one's thoughts or desires into realities has its source in Infinite Intelligence which knows more about plans than the one doing the praying.*

"Stating the case in another way, may it not be wise, when praying, to trust the Universal Mind to hand over the plan best suited for the attainment of the object of that prayer? My experience with prayer is a plan (if the prayer is answered at all), a plan that is suited for the attainment of the object of the prayer and material media. The plan must be transmuted, through self-effort action.

I know nothing about any form of prayer which can be induced to work favorably in a mind that is colored, in the slightest degree, by fear."

    We have a lot of different boxes for fear. Two of them are guilt and anxiety. There is guilt in living in the past and anxiety when living in the future. You can combat this with extreme presence. Being 100% committed to whatever it is you are doing now. You can even set time limits to limit your joy while you are getting started. If you are enjoying this book, and start to feel the guilt setting in for what you are not doing, set a timer and allow yourself to read for 15, 20, or 30 more minutes without the guilt. If you are suddenly inspired to work, while at home, and you have a moment to take 15, 20, or 30 minutes to dive in, 100% guilt free, do it.

Allow yourself to be more fluid. Allow yourself time to be inspired. When you can take this guilt free time for yourself, or your work, you can often walk back in with your family and continue to have guilt free time. Why should any time be associated with guilt?

It is quite silly the things we decide to deny ourselves. The simple pleasures. My God, why not enjoy that ice cream cone? If we have decided we are going to have it, have it. Why not enjoy work, your family, yourself? If you can't enjoy your own company it will be much harder to enjoy the company of others.

It is hard to enjoy our own company when we have believed the things we have been told about ourselves and internalized them. It is hard to enjoy work when we have believed so many lies about "work". Finally, it is hard to feel worthy of the family when we don't feel worthy anywhere.

We are unworthy at work, we are unworthy in our solitude, why would our families enjoy us? We are second place. We are subpar. They could have done better. This is the ego talking. The ego will be addressed later in this book. That big, brutal, awful bastard feeding you all the lies that keep you disconnected from the world. We will get rid of the ego simply by becoming less of what we are not.

Being in the moment becomes easier when you understand what a moment is and is not. It is not something to be encapsulated in a photograph. It is not pain stored somewhere in time to take out of our pocket and touched to make ourselves feel unworthy of the joy we are currently experiencing. The moment is always happening. It just tends to get sacrificed for the future.

I was asked recently to define success while sitting on a panel for the *National Association of Hispanic Real Estate Professionals* in Huntington Beach. I told the audience "success is profound gratitude for the present moment". What else do we have?

We will all find ourselves, from time to time, anchored deeply into a moment. The feeling that time will stretch on forever and simultaneously never move another minute. When you stop thinking about what you have lost, or what is to gain, but are simply grateful for what you have in that moment, you have found yourself in presence.

Napoleon Hill wrote "I now pray, not for more of this world's goods and greater blessings, but to be worthy of that which I already have." Through the ego we develop expectations for ourselves, for our families, and for our businesses. We often will let the world know our expectations and announce our expectations for ourselves. We will let these people know when they are not living up to our standards and we will call this "accountability". We will feel okay with letting others know they are failing because the person we are the harshest with is ourselves.

What if we tried something different? Instead of correcting the wrong note in the symphony praise the overall presentation. Instead of finding something to fault, find something to praise. Lynne Twist said "What you appreciate, appreciates". Haley Rushing writes in her article with the same title;

> *"The word Appreciation is a fascinating little word because it has four distinct meanings that all happen to relate to and support one another.*
>
> *To appreciate can mean:*
>
> *To be fully conscious of*
>
> *To hold in high regard*
>
> *To be grateful for*
>
> *To increase*
>
> *In order for what you appreciate, to appreciate you have to (1) open your eyes and become aware of it; (2) hold it in high regard; and (3) be deeply grateful for the joy it brings you. When you do that, it appreciates. When you don't, it depreciates."*

People often find themselves in abundance of the exact thing they don't want. Their mind is consumed with what they don't want, they think about it constantly, so they find it everywhere. Whether the thoughts are negative self-thoughts, about the business, or the family it is inconsequential. We should not function one way at home and another way at work.

The business world has their quintessential idea of what a loser is and they often refer to these losers during their presentations to illustrate a point. They talk about the garbage man, the guy working at the grocery store, the gas station, the fast food employee at the drive thru window, etc. and so forth. Most of these occupations I have held, or my mom has held, in order to feed our family or keep a roof over our heads. I have massive disdain for the word "loser" when applied to a human being.

I drove thru to get a Vanilla Cold Brew from *Carl's Jr.* recently. They are delicious and the line is always significantly shorter than Starbucks. The service was lightning fast but the entire time the staff seemed a little too rushed. The Manager was announcing drive times and orchestrating the flow of the kitchen. She seemed over-bearing and I am embarrassed to admit that, for a moment, I thought about complaining. I am so glad I didn't.

A few days later I drove thru again. The same staff was working but no one else was in the line. They were still quick but he seemed to have a moment to breathe so I asked how he was doing and he said "I'm great!" I asked why and he told me "We are the fastest drive thru in the region!" I didn't see a single loser in that kitchen. Not one.

Live your life now, be of service in whatever way possible, and know you are the right person for the job. Then do that job happily. We are above nothing and yet we are worthy of everything. We are worthy of our families, we are worthy of our businesses, we are worthy of this life, and we are worthy of our struggle. We are here. At any given moment you can say "I made it!"

We woke up today! What a fortunate group we are, we made it. We are worthy of *this moment*.

It is easy to get lost in a current struggle of the most severe degree, or of the most finite. Whether it is divorce, loss of a loved one, or loss of employment nothing is lost. Frankl writes in *Man's Search for Meaning;* "In the past, nothing is irretrievably lost, but rather, on the contrary, everything is irrevocably stored and treasured." We can give way to Nihilism, the thought that life is meaningless and without reason or we can cling to tragic optimism, the thought that life is beautiful and with meaning. I choose the latter.

A friend and past business partner told me once, when I was watching someone close to me die of cancer, "He has given you so many gifts and now he is showing you how to die." We can choose to lose everything with the loss of a dear friend, or a child, or we can know they lived with meaning, no matter the cause of their death. Though some of us will find meaning there as well.

We cannot be so concerned with the stories of our lives that we don't keep our pen perpetually placed to paper. Live with every stroke of the keys. Be exactly who you are and stop with what you are not. It is time to stop believing those things. We may not know where these voices started but we can decide when they stop and confront them when they reappear.

Treasured elements live on in new faces, are carried on in new hearts, and we can only hope the pain will bring us closer to the Source of Oneness. We spend far too much time trying to be worthy, traveling to salvation. What do we need to be saved from? Aren't these cages our own?

Move forward whole, and now, the best that you have ever been.

3. Zazen & Mushin: Meditation & No Mind

I have attended a fair amount of meditation classes throughout my life looking for something that "works" and have found many different options that guide us towards the desired feeling of peace and tranquility. Unfortunately, many of these methods are so overly ritualized that they prevent people from continuing on their own. Meditation is very simple; just take time to leave your mind alone.

There are great options out there for guided meditation, or concentrating on manifesting, as well as many other options but we are not going to discuss them here because most of those meditations have a goal or desired state. Meditation does not.

This is not to say these are not great options. When I find myself in a certain mood I have my own guided meditation and power pose ritual that I enjoy.

Transcendental Meditation is also a wonderful option, as are the other mantra mediations. If you already are using something you enjoy, great. My suggestion is to supplement these options with mini-meditations which help you to maintain a continued state of *Mushin* or "no mind" throughout your day.

Mushin is the absence of fear, anger, and ego. It is the ideal state for the warrior in battle, a businessman, or a parent at home with their family. When you have reached this state the mind works at a very high speed but without intention, plan, or action.

This is the state a great dancer may get into, a musician, or a presenter in front of a room. It is the moment the mind stops interfering and nothing is stopping you from acting in the now. When the guitarist hits an impromptu solo, his hands and his mind are connected with the music and the atmosphere around him. The notes flow through him and electrify his fingers. He is alive. He is aware. He is in a state of no mind.

When the dancer has rehearsed the routine to the point of muscle memory her body comes alive and no longer needs to think of the steps and because of this the movements are more beautiful to behold, graceful or sharp when necessary, and you can see in her face the feeling of the music washing over her.

We all have these moments when our training and life's experiences just help to color the experience we are having. Is training important? Absolutely! Training when paired with experience creates an expert.

The martial artist in a state of no mind is not the deranged lunatic, slobbering at the mouth. He is not the nihilistic warrior, who believes his life is meaningless, fighting idiotically without regard for himself or others. He is poetry in motion. He has trained so thoroughly that he no longer has to think about his training. The body and mind are one in motion.

We hear it referred to as "the zone". That special state we hold exclusively for professional athletes. It is not exclusive, in fact I think I have given you several examples of Mushin in action.

The best way to rid yourself of anger, fear, and ego is to realize when you see those ugly captors coming in to take over your moment. It is hard to recognize fear when you have never taken a moment to get acquainted.

Fear is nothing but a path guide whom we can reference as we see fit. We can take advice from fear but we must not let it rule us. When we know fear enough to be afraid of it, we have not grown acquainted enough yet. Follow your fears to their logical or illogical conclusions. Have a conversation with your guide and then, as the driver of your own body, make the decision to follow the advice or to keep going forward on your journey.

Anger is a harsh companion to keep fellowship with because, like fear, anger can drive you to accomplish great feats but when you make anger your master you will hardly find the ends justify the means. A surplus of pain and fear often hinds behind anger. An angry person is a fearful person, no matter how big of stature they may appear.

The ego is the great divider of all things. It is superiority and inferiority at work. It is removal of oneself from humanity. Any time we think we are too good for, or not good enough for, a moment the ego is at work. Men lose more money and opportunities to their egos than they have any wife, girlfriend, business, or divorce throughout history.

Meditation is a way to keep all of these things in check. When you can find time to clear your mind and be present you can catch yourself when you start slipping. For most of my life I did not know what presence was. In my opinion, this is something that should be taught in schools over most subjects we are teaching our children. It is only when we are present that we can rise above reaction into response.

There are a lot of excuses a person might present to get out of meditating and I will address them here:

"I don't have time to meditate."
- Do you have time to be in a bad mood all day?

"I'm not doing it right. I'm not good at meditating."
- Are you good at taking a shower? It is true that some showers will feel better than others but that doesn't mean a nice mental rinse doesn't help. Meditation is not an achievement, it is just taking time to leave your mind alone. It's interesting that the closest most people get to meditation is the time that they spend in the shower.

"I can't meditate for twenty minutes, twice a day!"
- Many people are great about waking up early and prioritizing their meditation. For others, it may have to fit in where it can. Whatever happens, don't be frustrated with yourself for missing a meditation. This is counterintuitive.

"I can't put on headphones, close my eyes, and light a candle all the time."
- You may be over-ritualizing your meditation. All of the incense, oils, and fragrances are crutches

for relaxation but they may actually be preventing you from truly meditating or ever reaching Mushin in your daily activities. Instead of connecting your desired state of mind with whatever activity is at hand, you will continuously be desiring performing activities that will help you enter your desired state of mind. Avoid the rituals, stay present in all things.

"I can't close my eyes for a long period of time."
- Then don't close them. The eyes should be open and looking at nothing in particular, or perhaps focused on a spot on the ground in front of you. You may feel compelled to close your eyes, this is fine. As meditation is a state of connectivity to the source of Infinite Intelligence and Oneness, closing your eyes may make you feel disconnected from your environment, which is in essence, you. Keep them open if you want to.

"I can't sit on the ground in the proper meditative position."
- There is no proper way for sitting when meditating. There is the traditional way of sitting, which I cannot perform due to a reconstructive surgery. You can sit, stand, walk, or lay down while meditating. The goal is to reach a state of Mushin when necessary as often as possible, no matter what position, or activity.

Over-ritualizing mediation is counterintuitive. It's like a relaxing bubble bath with 60 candles, flower petals, and soft music. It's nice every once in a while but someone had to put in the work, someone needs to watch the kids, and there are now 60 unsupervised candles lit. The expectations are high for this bath. It better be good.

There are many people that may look down on a state of "no mind" as stupidity, or not thinking, but it is quite the opposite. It is in *no mind* that we are truly free to move above technique and logic and in fluidity with everything around us. This is Mushin.

Now, really pay attention to what I am getting ready to tell you. It is very important. Try to focus. Immediately we sit up, we engage in eye contact. Maybe we lean forward to show we are paying attention. Can you pay attention *harder?*

We strain to work in ways we can work easily. We deny our intuition for sound logic and are surprised when our logical decisions pay off poorly years down the road, in all the ways we intuitively knew they would. There is a sixth sense we start to develop when we trust our gut; intuition.

Alan Watts gives the example of the heron catching a fish. The heron does not strain to see the fish, nor does it work to hear the fish, it is aware of the water. The heron is almost completely still until it smoothly goes into action, diving into the water and grabbing it's dinner.

In the Marine Corps we give the example *slow is smooth, smooth is fast*. When a person is working to go fast, they fumble, and they stress themselves out.

Instead, go smoothly. You may be surprised by how swiftly the task at hand is accomplished.

So, how do we meditate?

Meditation can be so many things! It may be easier to start by telling you what meditation is not. Meditation is not thinking about the past, however fond or terrible the memories. Meditation is not manifesting a better future or worrying and/or strategizing on how to create one. Meditation is taking an opportunity to, as Alan Watts suggests, "just leave your mind alone."

Meditation is not a ritual that must be performed to reach a desired state. The further you ritualize meditation, *Zazen*, the harder it will be for you to reach the state of no mind, Mushin, as desired.

Meditation does not require music, though music is a helpful aid which can be carried out of your meditation or turned on when needed to help key mental relaxation while performing other tasks whether complex or menial. That being said, music is an unnecessary crutch for meditation and can be another road block when wanting to reach Mushin later because it is an aid.

Let me explain; if in order to meditate I must listen to music, or wear certain clothes, or be in a certain room, or only at certain times of day, I will continue to meditate only while in this state. If it is only while listening to chakra music that I find myself in a meditative state, I will limit myself for the times it is available. Therefore I will not reach this state more readily throughout my day.

I prefer to sit down in an upright position, eyes rested but open and gently focused on a spot on the ground in front of me. I do allow my eyes to wander, aimlessly, at the trees or whatever is in front of me.

I rest my hands in my lap or take time to allow my hands to move freely, as I am autistic and stimming (self-stimulation) is relaxing for me. Simply allowing my fingers to rub against one another, or my hands to rub together, is very relaxing and helps me reach a state of no mind. One may say this is a crutch, and it is, but I also allow myself to stim pretty much wherever I am to help me reach a state of no mind or to allow myself to focus.

I place my feet flat on the ground but I will allow myself to adjust for comfort. Sometimes I will cross my legs, other times I will lean back in my chair. This is unimportant and inconsequential to my state of mind. Whether you are laying down, sitting up, or cross legged on the floor, just get comfortable and leave your mind alone.

If you find you have an itch, scratch it. If you find your mind wanders give it a moment and let it go. Let thoughts come in like cars passing by on a country road from left to right. Let them come by, drift by in front of you, and fade off into the distance. If you find your eyes drifting to nature, let them drift aimlessly. Do not contemplate the Nature of God, or think too deeply on the birds. Let the stone be a stone, don't make a sermon of it.

Observing nature, taking a walk, or watching the rain is a relaxing and meditative thing, unless you take steps to worry on the rain or be grateful for it. The rain does not fall for us, or for the trees, it just falls from a brief moment of separation, back into oneness.

Our thoughts are like the rain and when they fall into the ocean we become one. There may be waves and currents but the wave crashing ashore are no less a part of the ocean than calm waters and deep seas.

To meditate or not to meditate. Do it or don't do it. If you find you are trying to meditate, take a moment to laugh at yourself and let the rain wash over you. Take that shower. Take the mental rinse. Just leave your mind alone. Always thinking is always talking to yourself. Perpetually talking to yourself is insanity. Give it a break.

The ego hoards it's cup of water, holding onto great plans for making it into a lake one day. Releasing the ego is throwing your cup of water into the ocean. It doesn't take away anything that is you but carries you to places you may have only dreamed of.

Stop thinking and start seeing. Trust your intuition. Intuition doesn't have a reason. It just does it or it doesn't. It is a gut feeling. Act on that feeling. Release your plans and expectations and move freely. Reason is logical. It sees time and large objects. It sees a rock and to us "squishy humans", as Watts says, the rock is hard, large, and immovable. It's the same limitation we place on time. We decide in ten years we will have everything we need and so ten years is always ten years away.

If you must focus on anything focus on gratitude during your meditation. We are here! How fortunate we are to have woken up this morning. Life is full of chances and opportunities. In every opportunity we are worthy. We are above nothing, we are below nothing. The only difference is our state of mind.

We are worthy of the lessons in death and in the fleeting moments of life. Nothing is lost. Our treasured memories and our harsh lessons are retained. Feel the lessons and the treasures and disconnect from the pain. We do not need to hold pain like it belongs to us. What is the pain serving?

Wallowing in pain brings more fear, anger, and ego. It breeds more separation. Zazen is meditation. It's feeling nothing and thinking nothing but being aware of everything. You will not suddenly forget your obligations and appointments. You may just realize which ones are important to keep scheduling.

The first appointment of the day is with me and I do my best to keep my appointments. At about 6:00am before anyone wakes up, before I check my Facebook, or my email, or my revenue share, I make myself a cup of coffee and I sit down outside and I drink that cup of coffee and think about absolutely nothing and everything all at the same time, by myself, as the world wakes up around me.

I sit down outside, under the canopy, and I look at nothing in particular and try not to think on anything in particular. If my thoughts fixate, or stray, I clear them. I don't go scrambling for a pen every time a thought pops into my head. I just leave my mind alone. It will be busy enough shortly and I want to respond to the world around me.

I spend my mornings with me. I follow my meditation, more often than naught, with writing. With a clear head I work as often as I can in a state of Mushin. I am present. I am aware. I know what I know. I am trained in business and in life. I don't always have the answers and sometimes that is the answer.

It is through meditation that we let go of the ego and the need to be an answer, or to be the person to find one. We can let go of fear and anger and simply be of service. We cannot monetize being a good person but when we stop worrying about the money, just like happiness, it will come as a byproduct.

4. Detachment

We all have a story. Some sort of past we carry with us that helps us to define what we are moving forward. Unfortunately the stories we are telling ourselves, and other people, are preventing us from doing just that; moving forward. Most people go around introducing themselves based on their career and accomplishments. "Hi, I'm David. I am (this occupation) and this is how important I am." We have come to expect the speech so much when we introduce ourselves that when I don't give it to people they look dissatisfied.

More often than naught I just say "I'm David" when I am meeting new people and wait for them to tell me more about who they are and where they come from. I just listen. I'm not going to learn anything from hearing me speak and introductions seem stifling. I would rather have a conversation with the person than the career.

I let people talk to me about themselves and I listen. I hear about grandkids and production. I let them talk, even if I find I have sold more homes and they are very proud of the amount of homes they have sold. Why take this from them? I let people talk and ask them questions and I let them hear themselves talk. I tell relatable stories and encourage them to continue. Healing begins the moment someone feels like they are heard. Almost every week of my life people cry when they talk to me because they are healing.

People want to be heard and people want to be validated. Aren't we lucky that we get so many opportunities to do both on a daily basis? I talked so much to my wife over the past few years that my healing became inevitable. I talked about every reaction I was feeling, every past pain and present trauma, and every unexplained emotion within my body, until I started to feel less ashamed of myself and started to learn to self-regulate.

Helping a person to detach from the pain they are carrying and heal is less *hands on* than it is *ears on*. Be wary of the person who continuously keeps you coming back to them for advice. Be even more wary of the person that has you paying for it. Coaching, as well as therapy, depends on the continuous self-defeating thought that I am broken and incapable of fixing my own problems. I am defunct and deficient. How could I possibly possess the ability to make decisions for myself?

Coaching depends on manipulation of the ego. It is feeling better or worse about yourself based on outside influence. This keeps you in a constant manipulatable state. It is the gradual belittling of your ideas or discouraging you from trusting your intuition on your journey. The desire to plant the seeds of doubt within the client; do I know what it best for my business, my family, and for myself?

Coaching perpetuates the ego more than any other tool in any industry that I know of. It is fear, anger, and ego incarnate in one platform. There is example after example of fear based coaching platforms preaching winners and losers and worse; that you are broken.

Competition between broken people kept in a scarcity mindset.

I recently held a panel called *Empowerment* which was an all-female business panel with 10-minute tips on how to empower yourself, your business, and one another. It was the most powerful series of speakers I have ever witnessed in one room. It was dynamic. The Question and Answer session was powerful and the whole room left buzzing.

One of my favorite exchanges of the evening came from one of the speakers who debated an earlier point I had made when I said "you are not broken." She told the audience that part of the coaching platform she belongs to is that "we believe we are broken." I always enjoy a lively debate. I waited until she was done speaking and I told her I didn't believe she was broken. I believe she is a gift to this industry and we are all very fortunate to have heard her speak. I believe she has done more on her own, than most teams have accomplished together. I told her I couldn't possibly believe for one second that the person standing in front of me is broken.

There's a tremendous amount of job security in these platforms preaching to their clients and coaches how broken they are, when of course, they have the answers.

There are several other coaching platforms that lock their clients into long term contracts with penalties for cancelling and they sell them additional tools, packages, and retreats, and when the person can no longer afford to keep up, the excuse is always that they didn't buy more, try more, or do more. More broken thought is not the answer.

Are there exceptions to the rule? Absolutely! They are just few and far between. Greed has set in and it runs deep in the Western Business Climate. There are often broken men at the front of these programs not following the rules of their own platforms but selling the rules for you to follow. Street lamp prophets standing in the light preaching a certain lifestyle while their own homes sit behind them in the darkness.

The second we realize we are not broken the entire coaching industry will shatter. Mentorship and accountability will continue but monetizing the manipulation of people cannot continue when people wake up. There are often people on the tops of every business, industry, and platform reaping the benefits everyone else is being told to strive for.

The sentence "I am" needs no follow up. I am David. I am a Realtor. I am a writer. So what? **I am.** Of course, I identify as "David", and I work in real estate and write books, but putting those titles on myself are severely limiting. I am so much more.

We start to identify with our accomplishments and our careers so much so that we become these things. We hang them on the walls. We start to judge ourselves by whether we are on our way up, or are our best times behind us and we are past our prime and therefore past our use to this world, our industry, or our families.

We make plans to prevent the past from happening again and limit our futures because of the conditions of our past and then we limit hope. This is the most dangerous step in anyone's destruction and the closest they come to *complete loss*. It is when hope or faith must be pulled from within. This is when we teeter on the edge of nihilism and losing all hope or finding meaning and faith in the darkness.

Some people dive into stoicism and decide to spend life expecting the worst and being pleasantly surprised when no one around them dies that day. Spending an entire life planning for the worst is just as misguided as spending your entire life assuming only good things will happen to you. Detach from the expectations and be aware of the direction you are headed. We do not have to expect the worst in order to handle it effectively when it comes.

It is easy to think I am so good in trauma that I am designed for it. I might as well think everything out to its darkest conclusions so I am prepared when life punches me in the gut. This is one form of detachment but it misses the point in my opinion. There are many intelligent people that lived lives of stoicism. You cannot have the conversation without mentioning one of the most brilliant human beings to have walked this planet, Marcus Aurelius.

I do believe there was a time in history for stoicism. I don't believe this is that time. If we continue to dive first into embracing pain, we will find pain our constant companion. Whether we vocalize our complaints, or not, is not the issue. The issue is the color of the lenses with which we are experiencing the world.

There was another speaker that spoke on the Empowerment Panel who encouraged all of us to look for everything black in the room. She gave us 10 seconds to look at every black item in the room and then told us to close our eyes. My mind raced over every black item and I began to catalogue these items in my head so I could wow the room by how keen my observational techniques are; the chairs, the radio, the table, items of clothing people were wearing, specific sentences written on the whiteboard. After closing our eyes she asked what green items we could recall. Then she asked for pink and yellow and several other colors. I could not even recall that one of the presenters had worn a pink blouse.

We find more of what we are thinking about. This is why the momentary practice of awareness while releasing focus is so important. If you are going to choose to focus on one thing or another would it behoove us to spend that time contemplating pain or gratitude? What color lenses do you wish to see the world through? Some people may say "pink" or "green", while the stoics may answer "black". I would say "give me the clear lenses. I prefer seeing life for exactly what it is."

It is when we connect with one lens or another that we are setting ourselves up for pain. When we get connected to the "good moments" or the "bad ones" it colors our stories. When our pasts are colored in darkness, it is rather difficult to move forward to clear skies. We believe we have had such hard times!

I choose to look at no period of my life as "the good times" or "the bad times". I have no favorite year or best day and because of this I am free to enjoy each day for exactly what that day is, with no desire to paint it through the lenses of the past, or to see it for what it can be in the future.

I want to give you permission to tell your entire story one more time and then never tell it again, unless necessary as a way to connect to humanity. Tell all of the ups of how great you are, tell all of the terrible ways in which you have been victimized, and include all of the terrible things you have done. All of the worst of you. The stuff no one could ever possibly love. Tell it one more time to whoever you want or journal it out for yourself. Give the whole ego dump and be done.

The ego will tell all of the parts of the story that will separate you from humanity, your heart will tell all the parts that connects you to it. That is the difference between the ego telling a story and the heart.

There are a lot of people out there that don't think they have an ego because they think terrible things about themselves. This is more ego talking. This is more separation. If you think you are unique in your trauma or that your pain separates you from humanity, open a book.

Pain is not existence. It is often our key into healing and rising above an egoic existence which can place us into a state of Bodhicitta. Then we can move forward helping others to detach from their pain and heal in the moment. It is up to them to continue the healing.

The attachment to pain and trauma runs more deeply than our attachment to happiness. This is the reason a person can seem healed in one moment and the next morning they seem to have backslid into old patterns. They are attached to pain and trauma. It is part of their story and therefore a part of their being.

Don't worry about becoming better, or different, just become less of who you are not. The ego has fed us a lot of garbage about what we need to be in order to get where we are going. People use our egos to manipulate us into serving their needs. The ego is something you want to be in control of or at least be able to recognize in yourself. If you don't control your ego you can leave yourself open to being manipulated like a sock puppet.

The ego is at work in business. It wants to limit those beneath us and beat those above us. How can you want what's best for those that work for you if you cannot hope for them to someday outgrow your achievements? Every mentor should want better for the mentee than their own experiences or they should not participate in mentorship.

Peer expectations also keep us in an egoic cage. People in coaching constantly talk about being the average of the company they keep. They are always seeking to surround themselves with their betters with the hopes of outgrowing them and then someday "leveling up peer groups". This is a distasteful thought. Shouldn't you want the best for everyone around you, not just hope to continue to leave your people for better?

The goal in life, in any moment, is to raise your spiritual vibration to such a high level that others will feel your presence and be inspired to be awoken on a spiritual level and raise their own frequencies without you ever having to say a word or suggest a change to them.

You don't have to consciously level up your peer group. You only must concern yourself with tuning your own frequency and your environment will set itself into motion to bring your life into a new harmony. A harmonious life is impossible to attain for a person living in internal discord.

A myriad of things will happen in your personal life as new relationships, attracted to your new frequency, find themselves into your life. You will find more friends in passing throughout your day that are attracted to you. You will have developed your own gravitational pull of positivity. You will develop your own o-zone layer to protect you from negative elements wishing to crash into your life. You will orbit around bigger and brighter things and others will orbit around you. You have now developed an ecosystem for positivity and love to grow.

Old relationships will come around to be redefined. People raising their own frequencies will come back into your life and those lower vibrating people will either change or find your new energy detestable to be around. They will no longer have the desire to call you to help negativity fester in their own lives because negativity does not perpetuate in your own. They will raise their own or seek out others to perpetuate a lower vibrating lifestyle of disconnection, us and them, and pain perpetuated.

This does not mean life will be perfect but your perception of life will have changed significantly. The expectations of perfection will be less prevalent and so will the expectations of tragedy. There is less of a desire to take ownership for issues beyond your control and so you are free to respond to them if they even require a response at all.

Business is and should be a spiritual practice. The more we separate our business from our spirituality the more we will find discord within ourselves and a lack of spiritual harmony with our families and surroundings. It is often said "it is lonely at the top". What are you at the top of?

When we find ourselves out of balance we live fear based businesses. Fear is terrified of the outcome and so it controls and manipulates it within the best of its ability. Fear considers other people *force multipliers* of their own greatness instead of other people who have the ability for inspired thought long past the influence of fear.

It is okay to create systems and mentor. It is not okay to control your teams into success. Being a team lead is one of the most demanding and thankless jobs in the real estate profession. Most of these relationships between team lead and team member border on codependency while others jump fully into it with reckless abandon.

Most team leads think their job is to create mini-versions of themselves to do what they would do. Just like they do with their children. This is "mini-me". Your job, as a team lead, is to provide a space for someone to walk into their own greatness.

To brag about the agents that cleared $100,000 a year on my team, I would also have to tell you of all of my failures. To take ownership, or credit, for the success of my squad, also means that I will have to take credit for every agent that ever came onto my team, never sold a house, and left real estate disenchanted and frustrated.

I take ownership in my part; I was fortunate enough to be in the right spot to provide opportunities for other people to step into their greatness. As much as I fight my ego on this one, I take pride in the lives I was a part of during these years. I helped people believe they were enough. If only for a brief time.

I also carry a lot of lessons in failure and I am grateful for those too. The lessons that helped me learn more about my natural deficiencies I have to work to overcome. I do my best to drop my coping mechanisms and allow myself to live more presently and more vulnerably in every moment. It is important to note that vulnerability has brought me more joy than pain ever did.

Eventually you learn that it is only the walls built by the ego that prevent us from locking arms with every person we meet. We are guarded, they are guarded. There are so many walls to tear down. You can start by tearing down your own.

There are old principles which no longer serve us in business. There was once job security in building your DNA into your career. Now, I believe you should think of a career as something manifested, outside of oneself, which you are bringing to life. This may sound counterintuitive but allow me to explain.

The person who builds themselves into their career cannot disconnect from it. It becomes them, and so their failure becomes something that is worn. This is the difference between work and a spiritual practice. Not only should you disconnect from your career to become more efficient, you should disconnect from everything.

If we wanted to be long-winded but more accurate when introducing ourselves we should say "Hi, my name is David and my current spiritual practice is real estate and writing books." We would let people know our names and how we are currently serving humanity.

What's interesting is we would give a person weird looks if their business card read "David Serpa, Real Estate Spiritual Practitioner" but would have no issue with someone writing "Real Estate Consultant" on a card. Why? A person who is a consultant or a coach may consult you to the best of their abilities and interest while a spiritual practitioner would guide you beyond their abilities and in your best interest.

Someone may be reading, or listening to this, and thinking *coaching beyond their abilities... This Serpa guys is nuts!* If I were to mentor you beyond my abilities I would be open to two possibilities; first, that my intuition can be trusted or, in the very least, consulted and yours can too. Secondly, I could seek answers from other people with more experience without my ego feeling threatened.

The person who is their career limits those above them, and those below them, by perceiving them as such. Instead, they should be dedicated to the service of everyone. The person who perceives someone below will naturally want to keep them there and will even begrudge them success. The success will feel as if it was taken from them.

The person who perceives someone above, will be intrigued with seeing them fall, and may even dream of beating them. Instead they continue to beat themselves, or find they are losing to someone new. Others, who consider themselves below another, may withhold information or simply not perform within the best of their ability to act against the perception of being below another person.

Detachment from results will help you to honor your new momentary practice. You can enjoy heading in a direction without sacrificing the journey. Too often goals leave us sacrificing every moment between here and the result. Know what needs to be done and then stop limiting yourself.

Perhaps the hardest detachment to contemplate, and the reason I left detachment for the fourth chapter, is detachment from the family. I am in no way denying the necessity for my involvement in the health and well-being of my children. I just don't see myself as superior to my children and I can honestly say my children have changed me for the better. Most parents get to a place, eventually, where they allow their children to change them.

The moment you enter into a spiritual relationship with a child is the moment you apologize. Some parents wait until their children are adults to ever give them an apology. Other parents, never give their child the apology they are craving.

This isn't some large apology for being a parent and bringing them into this world. Apologies are like water on a landscape. Some children have a lush green, emotional landscape, because they have entered into a spiritual relationship with the person that gave them life. While others go deep into adulthood with a dry emotional landscape, coping the best way they know how because they have been made to believe they are not worthy of an apology. They are not equal to those around them.

I apologize when I am wrong. It is the first step in letting someone know you do not consider yourself better than them. The shame in hoarding these apologies and vulnerabilities from children is built in the parents own self-doubts and fear.

We see self-doubts and fear manifested in families where everyone thinks, looks, and acts the same. They have been offered the confines of love for which their children can exist. The borders in which love can exist. These borders are built in fear and control. Can you truly love something that is controlled?

Release control of your children and offer guidance. Have more conversations and give less lectures. Stop looking to create a mini-me and start celebrating your child's differences. This requires time and space to allow them to think for themselves. Most children don't get there. They continue into adulthood questioning themselves and living in fear of being different and ostracized for their pain. We shame them, by withholding apologies, and they wear it by thinking they are unworthy of the world. They will be perpetually peace-keeping. Peace is not always the ideal place for growth.

Another way to find yourself spending more time with your family and/or doing the things you love is to continue to become less of who you are not by participating in less of the activities that are not appealing to you.

Guilt often appears when we feel we should make an appearance at something we don't want to attend. The *shoulds* and *should-nots* keep us in the confines of peer expectation and we continue to live in self-denial to the grave. Do less of what you do not want to do, do more of what you want to do. This concept may seem selfish to a person who has not heard of it before but I ask you to stay with me.

Following all previous trails to their natural conclusion that all of your extra commitments and long work hours will bring you to a place of abundance. Now, in this perfect world you no longer have to sacrifice. What do you want to do with all this time and money? The first inclination may be I want to travel the world, I want sports cars, I want a bigger house. Then what? Then what? After all the cars and the traveling, what's next?

I had a beautiful conversation with a friend on the beach the other day. We have had similar paths and it was the first time I have heard my thoughts echoed back to me by one of my local friends or even one of my contemporaries.

He said, "if you would have asked me what I wanted to do with all the free time and money 15 months ago I would have had a different answer for you. I would have said 'sit around here.'" And he pointed out to the beach. He elaborated that at any given day it may change, but he desires to be of service now, more than ever before.

It is not in times of chaos but in times of silence and solitude that we ponder life's great questions. While questing for happiness it evades us. While searching for enlightenment it stays just out of arms reach. Dr. Viktor E. Frankl wrote "Pleasure is, and must remain, a side-effect or by-product, and is destroyed and spoiled to the degree to which it is made a goal in itself."

Detach from your expectations, your business plans, and your ego. Be cognizant of the direction you are headed in, place feet to pavement, be of service, and be prepared to receive. The more detached you are, the more confident you will be, and the clearer everything will become. You cannot smell your own nose. It helps to remain, intellectually, one step removed from oneself to see things clearly.

Detaching from your situation is giving yourself the opportunity to see it at a fresh angle. If you were to press your nose to a painting you might see smudges or even part of the picture but you will never see the whole canvas. Don't feel pressure to detach to such a degree that you will be able to take in the whole picture. This is impossible. We can tap into the source of Infinite Intelligence through solitude or conversation, but the blueprint does not belong to us.

The further we detach the more we can consider other angles of the painting. The more we experience life from all levels, the more perspective we receive. Some pick up perspective on the road. Others read books and take in the stories of others. While a few old souls come into this life having seen more than their time and carry the wisdom with them. To see this clearly just spend any amount of time around large groups of children.

Whatever your method of gaining perspective by detaching from your own story, it will only help you to see it more clearly the further you step away. Most of us do this best with the aid of time but the distance does not have to be physical in order for the lessons to be obtained.

Our severe methods we use to insist on attachment keeps old lessons coming to us until we finally learn what is packaged within. If the fear is homelessness, as it was in my childhood, the fear will continue to manifest in adulthood, no matter how secure or prosperous the individual.

It was not until I was ready to lose my house that I had any real ownership over it. I had sunk into a deep depression. The thought of returning to real estate evoked thoughts and feelings equivalent to returning to a life of prostitution. With the state that the world is in doing anything that didn't feel like service, left me feeling disingenuous. Especially something as meaningless as buying and selling real estate.

One day I called the bank and asked them what the cost would be to get my house current. They told me it would be a little over $23,000 and notified me my home had been entered into a state of active foreclosure as of that morning.

I sat with the thought of losing my home. I was already significantly in debt. I decided it would be okay if I lost my home. I decided I was not the number in the bank. I also decided I would prefer to keep my home and decided I would need to close four escrows in the next 60 days to have any hope in doing so.

My wife and I opened four escrows in less than two weeks and they all set to close in less than 30 days. It was immediate. Everything happened at once. Old clients, new clients, referrals. Over the next few weeks we would open escrows in three different counties and our ownership/revenue share check sky-rocketed to an amount that would pay the mortgage the coming month and both of the car payments.

The same thoughts can be applied to business. It was not until I was willing to lose my business that I had any real ownership in it. One step further; it was not until I was willing to lose my life that I had any real ownership in it.

You are not your career. You are not the money in the bank account. You are not the family you were born into. You are not your net worth. You are not your goals. This current moment is the sum of the experiences you have had multiplied by the amount of inspired action you have taken, divided by or multiplied by manifested thought.

The perception of success in our lives has more to do with the lenses we are wearing than the life that was handed to us or our current situation. It is only when we place our lives within the confines of a line graph that we can judge success. I can't speak for everyone but the type of success I am craving is unquantifiable within the confines of a line graph.

5. Bushido: The Samurai Code

"It is better to be a warrior in a garden than a gardener at war." -Unattributed.

We spend too much time fighting in this country to understand what peace looks like. We are taught from a young age to compete, to fight, to strive without giving us the understanding of what we are fighting for and so we raise warful people without reason.

Celebrating violence for the sake of violence, and heroism for the sake of having heroes, is causeless and creates severe inner turmoil within the celebrated and those celebrating. We maintain a sense of supreme nationalism within this country and it trickles into the minds of the people in our communities. The thought that one person is better than another.

We see this in the way our country, and its citizens, look down on people from other countries. We see communities that look down on one community while coveting another. It manifests itself it covert and overt bullying in the most extreme and discreet ways.

Overtly, we see it on a youth basketball court when an oversized child is throwing his weight around, needlessly, to cause harm to other children out of the eyeline of the referee. Covertly, it may be a gradual unrolling of a person's reputation, by spreading judgmental comments, rumors, or making mockery. Both covert and overt bullying depend on that sense of nationalism. We are better than you.

If this sense of being better than another person is not addressed in youth it continues into adulthood. People become product that can be bought and sold in the most severe ways. What you want can be taken by force or manipulated to your tastes. Human beings are put here to serve you, as you are better than everyone.

This habit of needless competition continues into the world of business. The big bully continuing to step on toes and throw elbows because they have been taught they are above the other person and above the rules. They have been taught that winning is the ultimate virtue and that the method for victory doesn't matter. Win at all costs and win big by complete and total destruction of your opponent.

Many might read these words and assume I am a pacifist or incapable of waging war in the business world or otherwise but don't assume I am peaceful because I forgot how to be violent. Being complicit is just as big of an issue as participating in these covert and overt ways of bullying and is just as distasteful.

I'm not urging you to participate in war but I am also not encouraging you to allow yourself or others to be bullied. There is a modern premise that Zen is a strictly peaceful and passive lifestyle but one of the founders of Martial Arts was known as the Bodhidharma, the founder of Zen. In fact, the term dojo means "the place where enlightenment takes place".

I'm not saying we are always at war, in fact we spend much more time at peace than we realize. Most of the war we are waging is internal. There will be people in your life that wish you ill, or even actively work against you. Some of them have the best of intentions, others do not. I have a sneaking suspicion we all have less haters than we think we do. And, when has hate ever healed anyone or helped anyone accomplish anything real or lasting?

The Art of War by Sun Tzu is a book on how to wage effective war, when to wage war, and how to manipulate and win the battle, in many cases without ever having to fight one. In the *48 Laws of Power* by Robert Greene we see several instances of battles won by staying many steps ahead of the opponent. Both books are necessary to read to understand the warful and power driven mind.

To be able to beat one's opponent, if possible, one should speak the language. In doing so, they may find they have no opponent. Either this opponent is unworthy of engagement, or the battle will be lost before it is waged. Other times, there is no cause for battle once an understanding is reached or the cost may be too great.

If war becomes necessary the time spent studying and learning the opponent will contribute to the ability to obtain Mushin, state of no mind, and will help one engage in defeating their opponent and negotiate the terms of peace, when the time comes.

I do have opponents. They are the captors of the unwillingly emotionally or physically enslaved. I have a strong desire to help people see and break the chains they wear. Unless they see and help break the chains themselves, they will find they are back in chains again. A physical manifestation of their emotional thought.

For those familiar with Bushido, you may sense a trend in my writing. Bushido is "the way of warriors" and originates from samurai moral values; "while also being influenced by Shinto and Zen Buddhism, allowing the violent existence of the samurai to be tempered by wisdom, patience, and serenity." (*Bushido, Wikipedia*).

There are causes for war or battles in today's Western Business Climate. Most of these wars can be fought with conversation and information. Most of them can be avoided altogether by detaching from the ego.

One of the biggest causes for unnecessary war between companies is comparative business. The concept that our businesses are comparable and should be stacked side by side with spreadsheets and bar graphs to quantify which one is better than the other. This is perpetuated in the real estate industry more than any other industry that I know of, but that is just my ignorance. I'm sure other industries are just as competitive.

We hear this line again and again "if someone gets business in your area of expertise, they are taking it from you!" Did they really take it from you or did they simply obtain business and it has nothing to do with you whatsoever?

This worked for me, it should work for you. That didn't work for me, it won't work for you. Spend more, win more, work more. Hustle. Grind. Sacrifice. I was guilty of some of this in my first book *The Machine Gunner's Guide to Real Estate; Accuracy by Volume.*

At the beginning of this chapter I used the quote "it is better to be a warrior in a garden than to be a gardener at war". In sticking with the analogy, concern yourselves with your own seeds and your own harvest and less with others and you will find it will suffice and be pleasing. Does the beauty of someone else's garden take away from yours?

Concentrate less on competition and more on what you can learn. You will find most of the best "competitors" have none. For years another agent in my office would "chase me". He would get upset when I would be given an award for "Top Team" in the office every month. He focused on beating me and only managed to beat himself. For the other 150+ agents in the office, they would have loved to beat him and come in second. For me, I wanted to beat the top agent in the region. If I had beat them, in that frame of mind, I would have then wanted to be #1 in Southern California.

Comparison leads to competition which leads to defeat and dissatisfaction. Who am I competing with? Who must be defeated? Comparative business is as toxic as comparative shame or suffering. It is gas in a room. If someone farts just a little bit in a room does it stink any less?

Dr. Viktor Frankl was a psychotherapist who survived the holocaust. Can you imagine complaining about your problems to him? But, shame must be heard. Our emotions must be understood if they are ever to be conquered. The only person worth conquering is yourself. When you have self-mastery conquered, elemental mastery will seem inconsequential.

Awareness is the gift of seeing what actually should be changed. Then you have a choice to respond to your surroundings and affect that change. If the samurai were warriors without ethics there would be no way to distinguish what *can be done* from what *should be done*.

Somewhere in my reading, be it Watts or Frankl, I read the *Statue of Liberty* on the East Coast should be complimented by the *Statue of Responsibility* on the West Coast. If we suppose that we are free, then what should we do with that freedom?

Vietnam Veteran Richard Pimentel gives a speech on *Goalcast* entitled *How to Live the Life You Never Imagined*. He recalls being given a speech by a leader when he was chosen to stay behind with that leader so that others may live. His wife reminded him of that speech when they chose to adopt four little girls so they could stay together. "Do we have the ability? Then, what is our response with that ability?"

What are your abilities? What will be your response with those abilities? Who will you choose to serve and how will you choose to serve them? This is the difference between servant leadership and management. Management meets minimum requirements to sustain employment. Servant leadership seeks the betterment of all, whatever that may look like, and the servant leader will use their abilities to help accomplish the task at hand.

A servant leader seeks to empower, build, and foster other leaders. They seek the questions they can quickly answer, find answers and solutions to the ones that take some time, and accept what they cannot. The ego is removed, or kept in check, and the business is free to manifest outside of the DNA of the individual. Sustainability is no longer desired and growth becomes a byproduct of movement.

The seven principles of the Bushido were set to provide moral ethical guidelines for growth of the individual samurai while effectively serving their masters. This code was later manipulated to glorify violence and kamikaze attacks at Pearl Harbor and there are several examples of samurai and their masters abusing their powers, but that is to be expected with any large organization with a moral code they are seeking to uphold.

The seven moral principles of Bushido are *Integrity, Respect, Heroic Courage, Honor, Compassion, Honesty and Sincerity,* and *Duty and Loyalty*. I will go through each one of these and how it pertains to the individual, the family, or the business if we wish to keep our *spiritual practice* alive and flowing seamlessly through all three, as essentially one.

Bushido

Gi (Integrity)

"… Believe in justice, not from other people, but from yourself. To the true warrior all points of view are deeply considered regarding honesty, justice, and integrity."

Don't lose yourself in expecting other people to be just. You cannot control justice and how it is distributed in all things. Always do the right thing for all parties and do your due diligence in representing your clients and yourself honestly and to the best of your ability. Win-win or no deal. We should not be here to "win" or take advantage but to serve humanity as ourselves. Consider, at the end of the day, most people are trying to feed their families even if they are going about it in a poor way.

Rei (Respect)

"True warriors have no reason to be cruel. They do not need to prove their strength. Warriors are courteous even to their enemies. …"

There is no "us" and "them" during a transaction or in life. There is only us. If you find you are working against someone, understand you are only hurting yourself. Revere all people and seek to serve them in the smallest ways, even if that is only with kindness.

Yu (Heroic Courage)

"Hiding like a turtle in a shell is not living at all. A True Warrior must have heroic courage. It is absolutely risky. It is living life completely, fully, and wonderfully."

Act now. Trust your intuition. Live life. "It is absolutely risky." But, what is the alternative? Giving way to fear and a desire for perfection will only paralyze your business. Just do it or don't do it but stop waiting for tomorrow to make the decision.

Meiyo (Honor)

"Warriors have only one judge of honor and character, and this is themselves. Decisions they make and how these decisions are carried out is a reflection of whom they truly are."

One of the best things you can do for yourself, your family, and your business is to disregard the expectations of your peer group. Most peer group expectations are toxic and don't consider individual situations or the individual. Besides, if you spend your life only making changes because someone else expects you to change, your change will not be made intrinsically. You are borrowing a *why*. Instead of committing yourself to internal and permanent change and building intrinsic motivation, a person kicks the can down the road and joins an accountability group or pays a coach to tell them what they already know to be true.

Jin (Compassion)

"Through intense training and hard work the True Warrior becomes quick and strong. They are not as most people. They develop a sense of power that must be used for good. They have compassion. They help their fellow man at every opportunity."

By constantly seeking individual improvement through training, emotional evolution, and perfecting one's spiritual practice a person is able to become more fully realized and effective in their areas of expertise. When they reach this state of enlightenment they are only interested in using their power to empower.

Makoto (Honesty and Sincerity)

"When warriors say that they will perform an action, it is as good as done. Nothing will stop them from completing what they say they will do …"

Many of you reading this book will have this trait already. We are like heat-seeking missiles once we acquire a target. Others tend to drift. Which is a rough habit to break. Drifters set intentions but find they are easily distracted along the way. This is why it is necessary to become aware of your values and then determine the direction you are headed. Be a heat seeking missile but stop letting someone else choose the target.

Chugi (Duty and Loyalty)

"Warriors are responsible for everything that they have done and everything that they have said, and all the consequences that follow. They are immensely loyal to all of those in their care."

It is okay to fail. Own it and learn from it. You do not have to carry shame with you to remember the lesson. You do not have to remind yourself of the ways you have failed. Be loyal to your team and don't expect them to be loyal to you. Do the same thing with your family. Then, do the same thing with yourself. It is hard to remember that momentary failures are learning opportunities with which we can immediately do better. When you recognize you are drifting, becoming angry, reactive, or egoic you are doing wonderfully! Don't shame yourself. Just take a moment to laugh at how ridiculous you used to be. You are aware.

6. Play

Do you play? What do you play? What is play to you? Too many adults "grow out" of playing. This is a shame! Especially when most of us have children who ask us to play so often. Give into play.

It is not too late to play. It is not too late to address your inner adult with your inner child. You will have to get uncomfortable playing until you break past your self-aware ego that is keeping you one step removed from play by worrying about coming off as silly or ridiculous. When did we learn to take ourselves so seriously?

This is one of the most devastating issues facing this country. Younger and younger children have stopped playing. They start mimicking older siblings and parents who exhibit egoic principles that keep them removed from their families, their businesses, and themselves.

What is play? Play is not *kind of pretending with your kids while checking the clock*. Play does not have a purpose or a deadline. There is no goal that must be accomplished with play. Do not play to work better. It is not another thing to be accomplished or another task to completed before the end of the day.

Whether you are playing with children, other adults, your spouse, or by yourself, it is important to get lost in play. It is also important that the play feels purposeless. The primary focus of play should not be getting paid.

There is no purpose to playing guitar. Playing guitar is purposelessness. Painting is purposeless. The second the artist starts worrying about getting paid for a piece of artwork or a song it stops being play. They are manufacturing. Writing this book is not play. It can certainly feel like play, at times, but it is not play in purposelessness.

Follow your bliss in play! Whether you are playing hide-and-go-seek with your kids, cards with friends, basketball, or idly strumming a guitar, it is important to allow yourself to drift into a form of "no mind" to give yourself the mental break you are craving without even realizing you are getting it.

When we get deeply entrenched in work stepping away feels almost impossible. Meditation becomes especially difficult. The mind does not want to stop thinking. The brain is finding solutions and working on overdrive because the mind is trying to survive. One of the best ways you can let your brain know that you are not fighting for your life is to take a moment to stop using it and play.

When you are playing the mind will fight to stay in control. After all, your survival depends on it! If you let down your guard and start playing, who knows what could happen? Take the risk. The mind will continue to want to be a part of the experience. It will over-analyze everything. It will feel guilty for playing, anxious about what needs to be done, or maybe aware of how good of a time you are having and then try to think you out of it.

As Alan Watts says, "Enjoy the pebble. Don't make a sermon out of it." Just play for the sake of playing. That moment is all that exists and all that is important in that time. Enjoy it. Enjoy playing with your children like this is the last time you might get to enjoy this, it is. Enjoy your own company like you may never get this moment to enjoy it again, you won't.

Music is purposeless. You do not start a song with the hope of getting to the end of it. If that were the case the person who composed the quickest song would win! Dance is purposeless. The point of the dance is not to get to the end of the dance, but to experience the dance. Play to play. Live to live. Breathe to breathe.

Why do the birds sing on a beautiful morning? Scientists may suggest that they are singing to attract a mate or are warning others of danger. Perhaps birds are much more Zen than these scientists who are putting them under the microscope. It might just be that they have it figured out. The point of singing is to sing.

We have put too many confines on play and because of that it has become harder and harder to find but it's easy to spot when you see it because it looks an awful lot like smiling and sounds like having a great time.

You should absolutely find time to schedule play, or at least prioritize it, the same way you do with meditation. Whether it is a weekly basketball game, playing music with your friends, going dancing, attending a yoga class, or having a day where you prioritize play with your family, make it happen.

Consistent play, like meditation, will help you reach a state of play while not actively participating in play. Just like how *Zazen*, meditation, is a state of no mind, and can be understood more thoroughly and slipped into with greater ease by participating in regular meditation. The mindset of play can be understood more thoroughly and slipped into with greater ease in moments when you are not currently at play by regularly engaging in play.

When you find you are slipping into making work play, do it! The joys of serving others will start to replace the dreads of work. Rejections will seem less harsh because you are, after all, just in a state of purposeless play. The point of the phone call is not to book an appointment but to have fun in serving others. If there is an appointment booked, what a fortunate side effect of play!

When you can find moments of play at work, play. If you can find yourself in service, while in a state of play, you have unlocked something beautiful within your heart. Of course there will be times when you cannot play and that is okay too.

It is only through regular engagement in joy, not in fleeting moments of pleasure, that we can hope to see this change within ourselves. Stoics should play more kickball. Some of the wisest people to have ever walked this planet were notorious for making points with humor, even if they were the first one to see the humor in the situation.

Play is beautiful, mindless, and silly. The ego can't stand it! The ego takes itself too seriously. It wants to win at play. The ego isn't good at play. You can't simultaneously be egoic and participate in joy. Joy requires presence and ego is façade.

Do something you are terrible at or have never experienced before just to completely shatter the ego! Play frisbee golf, go bowling, take a painting class. Don't do these things hoping for great accomplishments with your new found talent, or to ritualize your new joy and attach yourself to unrealistic expectations of play.

Play, like meditation, should not stress you out. If you find you are getting frustrated because you are missing your chance to play, you are doing it wrong. Just play when you can and try not to miss your day when you prioritize play.

We have believed far too many lies about work because they were taught to us by our parents, our coaches, or our teachers. *"Work isn't supposed to be fun! It's called hard work for a reason! Work to get ahead! Someday this hard work will pay off! My parent sacrificed so that we could eat and so I sacrifice for my children!"* And the cycle continues.

There is a great article on www.ZenHabits.net entitled *Work as Play* by Leo Babauta. In it he writes;

> *"I've discovered the concept of work as play, mostly because I've become my own boss, and can pick what I want to work on, and set my own schedule. As a result, I work on things that excite me, that I'm passionate about, and it's fun. If something is*

> *drudgery, I either drop it or find a way to make it play.*
>
> *As a result, I work harder than ever, but it's exciting and fun. I pour myself into my work, and can't wait to do it.*
>
> *Turning work into play doesn't mean you don't work hard, or that you never do boring tasks. If you've ever played a sport, you know that you work as hard as anyone when you're playing or practicing — but that's no problem, because you're having a blast doing it."*

I strongly suggest reading the entire article but, for me, the golden nugget came at the end when he addressed the coaches, teachers and parents, and bosses. Our job is to fix ourselves before we can ever hope to fix anyone else. The spiritual work that one goes through is a momentary practice and we cannot hope to guide others if we are misguided ourselves.

> ***"Coaches***. *Are you drilling skills into your players? Stop! You're teaching a game, so teach it by letting them play games. Let them play, but structure the play so it's not only fun, but instructive."*

This would go for a football coach, a basketball coach, or a real estate coach! Let them play. The worst thing we can do for a new agent or a new ball player is to weigh them down with rules and regulations. Free them up to learn without realizing they are learning; by playing the game.

The worst thing we can do for our young athletes, young actors, or a new professional is to drive them with fear. Fear and scarcity begets more fear and scarcity. Learning the game of basketball starts with a love of the game. Whatever is manipulated from there is the fault or the credit of the athlete and the environment they were fostered in.

Start with a love of the game not by paralyzing your team with fear. Too many coaches surround their teams with screaming men and foster competition over camaraderie and this is the beginning of the end of love of the game. The love is replaced with fear. Give them mini-versions of the big game that create success, teamwork, and camaraderie. The small, safe wins with the team will create the confidence to achieve the big, dangerous ones on their own.

> *"**Teachers and parents**. Are you drilling knowledge and skills into your students or children? Stop! Learning should be fun, and it really is when the child is allowed to have fun, to play, to explore, to create as he wishes, to learn about whatever he's interested in at the moment. Don't make it*

> *unfun. See the concept of unschooling*
> *for more."*

    We are removing room for inspired and creative work and replacing it with memorization and test-taking abilities. Public schools have gone the way of the industrialist and have strayed away from the creative intellect, which is unfortunate. Many charter and private schools have witnessed these trends and are reacting to it, while some public schools are doing their best to get their feet under them and respond within their abilities.

    By cutting art, music, shop, and theater we are denying the opportunity for children to shape their worlds around them by seeing their own manifested thought materialized.

    Our children are far too bogged down with homework and extra-curricular activities to experience free play and free thought. This is a direct reaction to our inabilities as parents to watch our children be bored. An entertained society has never been a virtuous society.

    We are going both ways quickly and we will make a choice between entertainment and enlightenment. Enlightenment is the beginning of peace for the next generation, while I fear entertainment will lead us rapidly towards destruction of a further generation, somewhere down the road.

    By loading our brains with facts and skills and then immediately being offered entertainment there is no time for idle thought. In idle thought is where a child first begins to experience awareness. While life experience helps bring about inspiration. They cannot become aware if they are constantly entertained, nor can they become inspired if they are always idle. There is a balance to walk and if we walk it in our own lives we will be more able to enforce it in our children's.

> *"**Bosses.** Are you forcing your employees to do drudgery type work? Do you control everything they do and when they do it? Stop! Give them freedom! Give them control over their work. Allow them to pursue things they're interested in. Google's 20% policy is just one example. When people can pursue things they're excited about, when they can turn work into play, amazing things happen."*

This is the difference between creating extensions of yourself in your employees and empowering them to attain greatness in their careers. If we perceive a person as below us we will be more apt to offer a schedule for them to live their lives.

I choose servant leadership. I choose to be, always, the right hand to the King or the Queen in front of me. When I am free of ego I have no desire to take away someone's rule in their own life, only to foster and curate their empowerment. This creates a beautiful domino effect of leaders creating leaders instead of managers grooming, and selecting a few for management.

With a growth mindset we are always open to developing a new team, a new goal, a new group of people to serve. With a sustainment mindset we are only interested in managing and conserving the business we currently have and our secretary will always be a secretary. This is not the mindset of most successful companies led by the True Warrior that is not threatened by the successes of others. Growth is the goal for everyone. If you are green, you are growing. If you aren't growing, what are you doing?

If we understand that our employees are more similar to us than different, and want to feel inspired to work, we will help them to create success without constraints and hopefully be pleasantly surprised when they think for themselves and see things that need to be done and do them without our asking. Far surpassing the expectations we would have set for them.

I have decided to create jobs for people and promotions for others because they saw something that needed to be done, and did it. How would that have ever happened if I had micro-managed every moment of their day?

> *"**Employees.** Is your work drudgery? Turn it into play! If you are stuck in a job where you absolutely cannot turn work into play, look elsewhere. There's more out there."*

Well said, Leo. Life is too short to spend it doing something you hate. What if life only existed today? How would we spend the rest of it? Would we go to another day of drudgery or would we spend our day elsewhere? Live your day in a way that you will be okay if you don't wake up in the morning but grateful if you do. We will get into this more later in the final chapters.

We have a choice to play today. We may have to work anyway, but we get to decide how we feel while we are there.

While you may believe you are too old to play, or that your children will not receive it from you, please understand that laughter is incredibly contagious, therapeutic, and healing. Many of the wisest prophets and teachers used humor in their parables to make a lasting point.

Being a serious person, incapable of play, does not make you wise. It makes you a serious person incapable of play. Wisdom and humor are not mutually exclusive. Find humor where there is humor to be found. Just exercise caution in expressing that humor. Not all jokes will make everyone laugh, and if they are at the expense of pain caused to another, or to their memory, it may be advisable to abstain.

Find time to schedule or prioritize play but feel free to jump into it at any given opportunity. How many times in your life will someone be vulnerable enough to say "will you play with me?" Don't miss these opportunities, too often, because you are working.

7. Stress

Living outside your meaning causes stress and anxiety. Find your peace by finding your place. While any career can be made into a spiritual practice you might find more natural joy in serving in a capacity that celebrates your gifts.

I fell into a place where I would say "I hate real estate" consistently. A bad moment had the propensity towards becoming a bad day. I was frustrated with the past and I was carrying it with me like luggage into the future. Instead of focusing on the gifts and joys of real estate and focusing on service and playing, like I did early in my career, I started sacrificing the day for tomorrow.

I have to remember there is nothing in my day I have to "get through". We fall into this negative habit by focusing on "the light at the end of the tunnel". We think, *if we can just get through this class, work, or appointment, then I can enjoy my day! I can finally relax!* Then, when we get to the moment where we are supposed to be happy, we find no happiness there.

We have set to sacrificing the present moment and so, naturally, we are not at ease. The ego is always working to get somewhere to be celebrated and when it is not celebrated it is in pain. You, the real you, wants to live in every moment. Your heart calls out for it! Your lungs crave that deep breath! Give it to them.

We believe everyone is doing better than us. Comparative business, as we discussed earlier, is toxic.

There is no need for a leveled up peer group expecting more from you. You are enough. Who do we need to compete with for happiness? If we beat them, will we get it? How long will that last?

The problem with expectations of peer groups and comparing lives and businesses with others is you are only getting a glimpse into their lives. Social Media has been great for giving people what you want them to see and withholding everything you don't want out there.

We are now able to present and feed the ego almost exclusively through social media. People spend more time celebrating their accomplishments than they actually spend time accomplishing. They celebrate themselves at every opportunity, put down others to their group of supporters, and present themselves as a pleasure seeker to model your life after.

Pleasure seekers want more money and time so that they may seek more egoic pleasures. Seeking validation without substance, building business without building character, and presenting illusions of service without serving. This is what I refer to as the street lamp prophet. Standing in the light of the street, preaching the answers, while their home sits behind them in darkness.

There are a lot of different ways someone's home can sit in the dark. Perhaps they are preaching business balance, yet have none. Maybe it is family and values they are preaching while their family may be more of a façade than a place they seek and give spiritual comfort. Maybe they preach peace while they are in regular inner turmoil. The Street Lamp Prophet is someone attempting to coach someone else into success they have not attained personally.

There are plenty of coaches and mentors who are well-intentioned. A select few are excellent. When a coach, broker, friend, or boss feels audacious enough to offer "work harder" as a solution to one's problems without being someone that has spent a season of their lives "working harder", it may cause an issue. If a person tells someone to "work harder" and they are successful in business but their marriage and family life is in shambles that may cause an issue. Following an advisor or receiving advice from someone who is spiritually out of balance will lead to being spiritually out of balance.

Just like how all homes have a smell, all homes and businesses have an energy. Collected and manifested energy is easier to feel than individual energy. Individual energy can be sneaky and allusive. Some people are like chameleons and have an ability to mask their energy.

You will walk away from many of these meetings feeling like something was "off" yet not being able to put your finger on it. Learning to trust your intuition is key. It speaks from a place tied to the Infinite Wisdom and often doesn't have a reason, just a feeling.

We go looking for answers in many of the wrong places. For every step you go outward, consider taking a step of equal or greater size inward. Without taking the time to understand ourselves, our temple, or our home, our journeys outward will feel empty. We will continue to feel spiritually homeless.

When we are spiritually adrift the answers always seem external and we mentor people to feel the same way. We give advice on one aspect of our life, which we feel we have mastered. Even if all the other areas around the business are feeling out of balance the world is still applauding so we teach other people to seek the applause of the external world.

When spiritually sound, we know there are no answers outside of ourselves. We are less apt to offer the answers to others. That's not to say spiritually sound people do not give advice, however, these people have no egoic or vested interest in your story. They will let you talk and ask questions so that you may hear yourself come across the answers.

Too often the stress we incur has less to do with the external world than it does our internal world. When we can't fix our own problems, or they seem insurmountable, or boring, we will focus on someone else's problems. It's a nice thought but imbalanced people can't help imbalanced people find balance. It is more likely they will unintentionally pass on versions of their own problems. After all, this is advice coming from someone that is "successful" and "has it all figured out" so it is more likely the advice will be followed.

Seek counsel, if you must, but make your own choices and act on them. You will be the one to walk down the road you choose. There are many reasons others have to influence your decisions. None of them belong to you. They consider their own paths, shortcomings, or strengths and apply it to their limited understanding of you.

In business and in life we seek to control the outcome. I wrote earlier that it is good to set intentions and take inspired action and then understand that it is best if the entire plan doesn't belong to us on how to attain these things. We must only act one move at a time. If our moves are intentional and inspired we will enjoy the journey and more gratefully accept the outcome or next step in the journey.

One step further; there is no outcome. Every failure is only momentary. Every failure is perceived. Just like every win. Part of our problem is that we keep waiting to arrive at a finish line where we will have all the time, money, and recognition we need. Of course this will continue to allude us. This is why so many people say things like "this feels like a huge setback" or "I have traveled so far, for this to happen". Where are you going? What is this destination?

The same people say "I am so sick of fighting". Who are you fighting? Why must they be fought? Is it possible your mission could be accomplished not by fighting the opposition, but by simply accomplishing the task at hand? There are no demons to face, there is no one to fight. No one must be beat in order to be a more joyful and grateful person. Gratitude is not stolen. Joy is not something that can be lost or received.

It is only natural to want to control the outcome. Control is asking for the plans, while surrender is admitting you don't know how you will get it done, or if it will get done, but working towards that direction like it's already yours. I hated the idea of surrender. It seemed like a dirty word, synonymous with defeat.

Many of us had childhoods, or have lived through situations, where our lives or livelihoods have been threatened and we feel that fear served us through these situations. Thank your fear for everything it has done for you so far and allow it to advise you from the passenger side. Let love take the wheel. When intuition guides you it will feel like love and it may not have a reason. When you are guided by fear, it will sound very logical, and will offer you a hundred reasons. Who will you listen to?

Many people spend their lives seeking permission to live them. We ask everyone else's opinion but don't seek our own guidance nearly enough. It wasn't until I was willing to lose my house that I had any hope in saving it. We are not these things.

No one could ever hope to understand you the way you understand you. When one intimately understands their instrument it frees them up for mastery of it. Stress becomes harder to come by. Now you see obstacles without attaching the negative emotion to them. In fact, in a state of Mushin, we don't even have to see the obstacles, just be aware of them, to overcome them.

There is no shortage of stories to choose from when it comes to a person saving themselves by cutting into their own body. There is an article entitled *Top 10*

Incredible Self Surgeries on ListVerse.com that gives us example after example of people that made the decision. Amanda Feilding took a dentist drill to her own head to perform a trepanation, Aaron Ralston amputated his right arm when he got into a hiking accident, and Ines Ramirez performed a successful Caesarian Section on herself after 12 hours of laboring alone.

      The reason has to be big enough, the discomfort so great, that we are willing to cut into our bodies and leave a piece of it behind. The pieces that no longer serve us; fear, control, ego. It is a scary thing to attempt to live a life without all these coping mechanisms we have deemed necessary for survival, or have repurposed to serve us in the business world, but it is a worthy venture.

      The body will continue to be in a state of stress as long as we continue to believe we are not enough. We will take others fears and make them our own. We will disregard our own intuition for others logic and resent them and ourselves for our inability to move in the direction of our soul's stirrings.

      This may be an oversimplification but I believe there are two types of people that set out to heal the world; the first believes, on some level, they are broken and that their service will somehow make them whole. They concentrate on the world's problems because their own seem too difficult or painful to tackle. The second knows they are whole and sees their own pain as a way to connect to, and heal the world. Neither is wrong, but only one is living in fear.

This story is from *Simple Mind Zen* entitled *Nasrudin: The Lamp and the Key*. It follows Nasrudin, a Sufi teacher notorious for using humor to illustrate a point.

> *"His friend, Mansour, comes to visit him and sees Nasruddin on his hands and knees, crawling on the sidewalk under the street lamp, obviously searching for something, appearing frustrated.*
>
> *Concerned for his friend, Mansour asks, "Nasruddin, what are you looking for? Did you lose something?*
>
> *"Yes, Mansour. I lost the key to my house, and I'm trying to find it, but I can't."*
>
> *"Let me help you," responds Mansour. Mansour joins his friend, kneels down on his hands and knees, and begins to crawl on the sidewalk under the street lamp, searching.*
>
> *After a time, having looked everywhere on and around the sidewalk, neither Nasruddin nor Mansour can find the lost key. Puzzled,*

Mansour asks his friend to recall his steps when he last had the key, "Nasruddin, where did you lose the key? When did you last have it?"

"I lost the key in my house," Nasruddin responds.

"In your house?" repeats the astonished Mansour. "Then why are we looking for the key here, outside on the sidewalk under this street lamp?"

Without hesitation, Nasruddin explains, "Because there is more light here . . . !"

    Nasruddin, in this story, is making light of our desires to go looking for the answers in the brightness while leaving our homes behind us in the dark. Much more of our answers lie within us than we care to admit. I'm not suggesting to go kicking over every stone of your past looking for problems to unearth but rather allow yourself to move forward with the lessons you have learned while leaving the pain behind.

    I believe Eckhart Tolle also shares this story in *The Power of Now* and he suggests not just being a seeker of answers, but also allowing yourself to be a *finder.*

    It does not serve us to carry pain and yet we do. We carry it to prevent ourselves from feeling pain again. Instead, we are only capable of feeling pain. When we cloak ourselves in pain we will never be able to tap into all of the self-love that is waiting for us. It takes courage to live your life vulnerable to experiencing each moment.

     Make the choice to walk bravely into your home and start looking for the key. I don't know what the key unlocks, but I think you do. Remember, there is more courage in giving an apology than demanding one. There is also tremendous courage in knowing you do not need an apology. We can forgive them anyway. Why would you ever need someone else's permission to forgive them and be whole?

     There are times we will feel stress or discord when we are working towards enlightenment. Enlightenment is not something we quest for, it is a by-product of understanding the wholeness of everything and then being intentional in ascending. It is momentary.

     There are two types of stress that we will feel in our lives *eustress* and *distress*. Only one of them is beneficial. Eustress is defined as "moderate or normal psychological stress interpreted as being beneficial to the experiencer." Whereas distress is defined as "extreme anxiety, sorrow, or pain." Distress often comes from connecting pain with time.

     Think of your body and mind as an instrument. You could even take one more step and think of your body and mind as the music coming from your instrument. Currently, the music world tunes to 440Hz.

This is considered standard tuning. This was not always the case. Much of the world tuned to 432Hz.

Many of the greatest musicians like Mozart and Verdi based their music on the natural vibration mathematically consistent with the universe. The article on *Attuned Vibrations* explains;

> *"Music based on 432Hz transmits beneficial healing energy, because it is a pure tone of math fundamental to nature... It's true that it is only 8 vibrations per second different from the standard tuning, but this small difference seems to be remarkable to our human consciousness."*

> *"According to Ananda Bosman, international researcher and musician, archaic Egyptian instruments that have been unearthed are largely tuned to A=432Hz. Ancient Greeks tuned their instruments predominantly to 432Hz. Within the archaic Greek Eleusinian Mysteries, Orpheus is the god of music, death and rebirth, and was the keeper of the Ambrosia and the music of transformation. His instruments were tuned at 432Hz."*

When you are raising your vibrations there will naturally be some discord. You are tuning up to a new frequency. The stretching of your life's strings will feel therapeutic at times and other times extraordinarily painful. You can play an instrument where it is mostly in tune but it will not sound right. You must tune your whole instrument.

Every musician knows that their instrument requires regular tuning and maintenance. You can keep playing for another song, or two, but sooner or later you will have to stop to tune. Keeping your instrument in tune is regular maintenance.

You can also go through an entire lifetime playing and listening to music in standard tuning and never know the difference. If you decide to raise your frequency you will experience discord along the way as your environment adjusts itself to your new inner frequency. Keep working towards harmony.

Every person functions on a certain vibration. A person can raise and lower their vibration throughout their lifetimes and even throughout their days. Only crazy people instantaneously change their vibrations consistently.

A higher vibrating person can, momentarily, be affected by a negative vibration causing them to temporarily lower their frequency and become reactive. However people with high frequencies are less apt to become reactive and backslide into lower vibrating habits.

It is often easier to recognize distress in the body first and then trace it back to your mind and find the source of the problem. Distress causes discord and if we are not careful we will fall into old habits destined to repeat old patterns.

Unfortunately, it is only in moments of distress that we can make the choice to ascend above our current programming and work towards real and lasting change. If we are only living lives of enlightenment when we are surrounded in peace and tranquility then how extraordinarily fragile and useless our enlightenment is!

Enlightenment brings about awareness. Awareness is seeing things as they are, not as you wish them to be. With awareness comes a desire to effect change in the heart of the True Warrior.

The True Warrior walks the path. They do not concern themselves with whose path they are on, or what company they share along the way. They only know that this path is the necessary one for them to walk down, at this time, in order to get where they are going.

When you are walking your own path you will concern yourself less with anything other than performing your necessary duties. You will seek out who you must, and others may seek you out. As long as you do not lose awareness you will not be distracted by unnecessary deviations from your path. The True Warrior will stop to help the destitute or stranded, when possible, but will not lose track of the path and will not give more than they can in order to keep going where they are going. What is the mission? Why must this mission be accomplished?

If you can answer these questions for yourself you will find your *why*, without feeling it necessary to borrow someone else's. Friedrich Nietzsche said "He who has a *why* to live can bear almost any how."
Are you living your why or are you borrowing it? If your why is as shallow as money, every problem will seem insurmountable.

Developing a lifestyle brand is essential for the heart centered business. Service oriented people must feel confident in themselves and their product and see the need in order to believe they are serving by providing the product and/or service. If not, the business will either fail or become egoic and celebratory of egoic principles. Egoic businesses are fear based businesses. They celebrate the ego because the only thing behind it is fear and pain and who wants to celebrate these things?

When you raise your frequency bad energy is repelled. It will attempt to lower your frequency to maintain its harmony, it will adapt, or it will leave. Negative energy can't stand positive energy. We have all been in a bad mood when someone else is in a good mood. Their good mood seems to frustrate us more. We attempt to "harsh their vibe" and bring their frequency down. We bait them into fights. We bring up old pain points or unresolved issues and we seek to claim their good mood. If we are unsuccessful in our attempts, we leave, or we adjust ourselves and eventually find we are in a better mood.

Stress is simply discord. What is causing you to be out of harmony? I won't make you answer that one. It's just you. The ego will feel attacked by this one. *I am not the cause of my problems*, it says. It will seek to manipulate the words, as manipulation is crucial to the survival of the ego. The ego cannot survive in naked truth. You are not the cause of all your problems but you are responsible for how you respond to them and the light in which you paint them.

Walk bravely into the darkness of your own home, flick the light on and find the key. Take a moment and look at yourself in the mirror. Be grateful for the person that stands before you. This person that was courageous enough to walk back into their home and claim it, once again, as their own.

Do not judge yourself for the things you have done or said before this moment. Think of yourself as a child, even just a few moments ago. Now that you are aware, what will you do differently?

8. Principles of Zen Business

Throughout the course of my writing career and in this book I have touched on Zen Business Principles which I would like to expand on further. These principles do not necessarily warrant their own chapter but are, just the same, necessary to expand upon.

This work would feel incomplete without the mention of these principles.

Efficiency

There will always be those with a strong desire to 10x everything around them. I can say this was not a lifestyle that was conducive to joy for me. My first book was *The Machine Gunner's Guide to Real Estate; Accuracy by Volume.* It is a book that wears pain, ego, and trauma on its sleeve.

I have looked at business through the lenses of war for quite some time. There is a lot to learn from military tactics that can be applied to business. War has shown me a lot about life and I am grateful for the lessons. One of the main lessons I took away from war; we spend much less time at war in our day-to-day lives than we think we do.

It is easy for the neurotic or fearful person to feel attacked as they spend much of their days attacking themselves within the confines of their own heads. This is why many bosses or team leads can't receive input. They feel their egoic claim to the chair will be tested if they were to look to others as their equals and receive input. They work to keep those perceived as below themselves, below.

Every business event I held I threw extravagantly over the top. I included my team on everything but I ran my business in an *us against them* mindset. It was my team against the world and because of this my team had enemies in the form of competition.

I looked at much of the business that I missed out on like I missed out on it. I took every listing sign that went up without my name on it personally. Every open house sign out in town, without my brand on it, was the enemy.

Let me make this clear; my team and I never acted against anyone. We just talked about other teams and brokerages with a hint of condescension. We were very good, very popular, making a lot of money, and getting a lot of recognition.

We were #2 in our region of 4,500 Realtors for three years running and we all wanted to beat the #1 team. Harboring animosity is like drinking poison and expecting the other person to die. After three years of chasing the #1 team together, my top three agents left my team and joined the #1 team. Dealing my egoic business the death blow I needed to reconsider how I was running my life. What you resists, persists. What you appreciate, appreciates. I needed to do less of the former and more of the latter.

As much as I respect Grant Cardone and his *10x* mindset, I don't believe it is a mindset that works for most people. Looking at life like some sort of competition will always leave you competing and it will prevent many from living in the present moment.

I have traded in my machine-gunning accuracy by volume mindset for one of efficiency. This decision does not exclude battleground tactics but rather enhances them for strength over time.

When the mission is to *win a firefight* accuracy by volume is important. You send as much led accurately down range as possible. When the mission is to win a war accuracy by volume still would work if you have superior funds, weaponry, and manpower. In both the battle and the war the accuracy by volume mindset can create long-standing and unnecessary animosity from the losing party and the surrounding area.

Efficiency is king. Why fire 200 rounds when you can fire 10 and get the job done? Why continue punching another person once they have been knocked out? Why put 16 open house signs on one street corner when 3 would suffice? People conduct their businesses with the same lackluster performance and grace of a street fight.

The True Warrior does not overstrike. Overstriking causes resentment and backlash. By only exercising as much force as necessary the expert martial artist shows their grace, intelligence, and mastery of self to the people around them and to the person they are fighting.

There is something to be said for hitting the ground running in the beginning of your career. I have said several times before *success is very difficult to attain in a state of balance.* Most successful people I know, including myself, 10x'd their careers at some point or another.

I no longer believe this is necessary to attain a certain level of success relatively quickly. I still believe in hard work, I just don't believe that it requires sacrifice. We can practice spiritually with our families, our businesses, and ourselves without the burnout. Just focus on being of service and the rest will come.

The problem is that we don't know when enough is enough because we are continuously told "more is the answer". There comes a time when it becomes excess and fear takes over. For me, the tipping point was when I went from 11 agents to 28 agents. It was simply too much for me to handle without developing more systems or hiring additional staff.

I really had no interest in growing. In fact, it caused me a great deal of stress but herein lies the problem in following the expectations of your peer group. It just seemed like the next thing to do; get bigger, make more money. Everyone was constantly wondering; what's next? When are you going to hire again? It was never enough.

There are two different types of ways to launch a business in the beginning; the snowball or the avalanche effect. The snowball is the traditional way to work and certainly most reliable. It depends on getting on your hands and knees and packing together a small snowball to start. Continue to scoop up snow and add to the size of the ball. The goal is to eventually get the snowball so big that you might push it down the hill and it will continue to get bigger. This is the snowball effect.

The other way to generate business is the avalanche effect. This is easier to do when you have some clout, see a need, or have developed a more intelligent way of doing something. This requires less grunt work and maybe more intellectual work building out the initial foundation for the plan. The goal with the avalanche is to strike at a couple of key points and then hopefully let all the snow come flying down the hill towards you.

The problem with most new business owners is they are trying to use the avalanche effect without the clout or the knowledge. They spend all this time, energy, and money preparing the perfect business and never put in the work to launch it. Or when they finally do launch they realize it will not work the way they have it set up and they have spent far too much time in preparation to continue with a new plan before they quit.

The problem with most experienced business owners is that we continue to use the snowball effect to generate or grow new business opportunities long after having the clout and the ability to place a couple of sticks of dynamite and allow the avalanche to come down the hill.

Presence

We have talked about presence a great deal in this book. We have also talked about not having goals, or a business plan, but trusting in yourself and your intuition to know the next best move while being aware of the general direction you are headed in.

In my last book, *All The World's A Stage: Unmasking Asperger's Syndrome* I wrote about the *Power of Present Goals*. It is important that our goals are momentary so that each victory and failure is momentary. Having momentary goals allows us to snap into self-awareness and make adjustments.

Setting a ten year goal is the most worthless practice in business. Having goals that are ten years out will perpetually keep them ten years out. Ten year goals, believe it or not, are self-enforcement of limiting beliefs and are enshrouded with egoic desires. How many of your ten year goals have you accomplished? What about your five year goals?

The problem with ten year goals is they cannot be broken down into bite-sized pieces. There are many real estate coaches that are rolling their eyes right now and *thinking I would just break them down and work backwards.* The problem with this is; you don't have any idea what is going to happen next year! Life is what happens while we are busy setting goals and making plans.

Instead of working backwards from ten years from now based on what you think you might want when you get there and sacrificing every moment between now and then, act today based on the life you are currently living.

I developed these goals to give us momentary reminders of our successes and failures. If we can fix our now, the joys ten years from now will be a ripple of the joys we are experiencing today. Positive drops in the bucket send positive ripples throughout your life and into the lives of others. Negative ripples do not create positive ripples in the future. Therefore we must be cognizant of the pebbles we are dropping in the water in every moment.

Present Goals

Here are ten present goals to help you attain momentary victory over yourself.

1. Have goals you enjoy traveling to, not just arriving at.

2. Be present in all things; with work, people, family, and self.

3. Be a tuner of humanity, not a cause of unnecessary discord.

4. Give love freely, without expectation of a return of any kind.

5. Live life as if. Be who you want to be now. Stop waiting.

6. Live life freely. Without the confines of guilt that comes with living in the past or the anxiety of trying to control the future. Life is now.

7. Choose to respond to stimulus not react. I will find grace, intelligence, and dignity in the moments between the stimulus and the response.

8. Choose Love over Fear in all things.

9. Hear the words behind the words by taking the time to listen.

10. "If you want to change the world, go home and love your family." - Mother Teresa

Self-Reflection

The *Three Sacred Treasures of Japan* are Kusanagi (the sword), Yata (the mirror), and Kagami (the jewel). The sword stands for valor, the mirror for wisdom, and the jewel for benevolence. The mirror was said to have been the most sacred as it allows the person holding it to see themselves as they truly are.

Awareness

Just as it is important to see and understand yourself with clear eyes, it is important to see and understand your surroundings with accuracy. It is not enough to see the world as you wish it to be, or as others wish for you to see it, you must first accept it as it is if you should ever hope to effect lasting positive change.

Breath Control

    I wrote extensively on breath control in *The Machine Gunner's Guide to Real Estate* and the epiphany I had while listening to my daughter breathe while sleeping on my chest. I picked up the trend of breath control during shooting practice in the Marine Corps, in martial arts, and in yoga and started to apply my basic understandings to my life and parenting. The desire to keep myself in a responsive vs. reactive state. This way I can respond to my surroundings with grace instead of reacting to them to the best of my current and distracted ability by applying intentionality.

    My daughter's breathing was a little shallow. Perhaps she was having a nightmare. I took a moment to regulate my own breathing. I took deeper breaths, and so did she. She relaxed into a deeper state of sleep with both of us taking deeper breaths together.

    If a person is working themselves up into a state of anxiety and you remain calm and continue to take deep breaths, they will eventually relax. They will be soothed by your presence even if very little is said. However, if the person is anxious and you greet their anxiety with shortness of breath and quick movements while speaking without considering your thoughts, you will both find yourselves in a state of shared anxiety, anger, or even frustration with one another.

    If you can control your breath you may not be able to control your surroundings but you will be able to control your response to them. Sometimes the best response is no response at all. With a general awareness and deeper breath the world will feel different because you are no longer worried about what must be reacted to but you will be aware of what must be done. You will spend less time worried about the angry driver on the road. You will be aware of your safety, and those around you, but will understand what requires a response and what does not. You will also understand how little anger is necessary.

In the article *The Power of Breathing: 4 Pranayama Techniques Worth Practicing* published by *One Medical* Allison Hodge describes pranayama and gives four techniques designed to bring sleep, cure anxiety, help you wake up in the morning, and cool you off at the end of the day.

> *"In yoga, we refer to this as pranayama. 'Prana' is a Sanskrit word that means 'life force' and 'ayama' means 'extending' or 'stretching'. Thus, the word 'pranayama' translates to 'the control of life force'.*

I prefer the exact translation "stretching or extending of the life force". The only control comes in the response. Controlling the expansion of your life force is counter-intuitive. Instead, just open your life force up to indefinite expansion. Leave control to the people that are still building dream boards and drafting business plans.

Purposelessness

We get too lost in finding our purpose or serving the greater purpose and, because of this, there are times we can feel insignificant or lost in the greater sense of things. Do good anyway. Do good when no one is looking. Make the right choice. Do something that feels good just because it feels good not for the validation it will bring. A kiss can be a great thing to give or receive but it was also a kiss that Judas gave to Jesus that brought about his arrest and crucifixion and the insanity of Judas himself. Don't worry about the kisses you have received and what they meant, still give them.

You cannot control the outcome. You cannot control the world. You can only control the outlook. Mother Teresa said;

"People are often unreasonable, irrational, and self-centered. Forgive them anyway.

If you are kind, people may accuse you of selfish, ulterior motives. Be kind anyway.

If you are successful, you will win some unfaithful friends and some genuine enemies. Succeed anyway.

If you are honest and sincere people may deceive you. Be honest and sincere anyway.

What you spend years creating, others could destroy overnight. Create anyway.

If you find serenity and happiness, some may be jealous. Be happy anyway.

The good you do today, will often be forgotten. Do good anyway.

Give the best you have, and it will never be enough. Give your best anyway.

In the final analysis, it is between you and God. It was never between you and them anyway." -Mother Teresa

Enough

There is enough, you are enough, that will be enough.

There is enough! We have no reason to compete with one another. There is no need to take anything from anyone. I used to get frustrated when people would copy a marketing piece, an event, or teach my scripts without giving credit. Now, I have no issue whatsoever with these things.

You are enough! You are whole and complete now. The best for the job and ever-growing. If you are green, you are growing. Do not let anyone tell you "you are not enough" and certainly don't pay them for it.

That will be enough! Stop beating yourself up, stop beating them up, stop looking for something to beat up. Adjust your body and mind for peace and then be ready to receive it.

It is only scarcity that keeps children going to bed at night without food in their stomachs, clean water to drink, and a roof over their heads. It is only fear. If even half of us were willing to choose love above fear, despite the consequences, there is no telling what we could accomplish.

9. Die Before You Die

> *"I shall pass this way but once; any good that I can do or any kindness I can show to any human being; let me do it now. Let me not defer nor neglect it, for I shall not pass this way again."*
> -Etienne De Grelle

You do not perpetually have to be in a state of service to be enlightened. Sometimes you just have to enjoy the cigarette. Zen could be something as simple as enjoying a vice vs. punishing yourself for it. Why should a guilty pleasure be guilty? Wherever you are, be there, and *live and die* in every moment.

If we are on a diet and have committed to having an ice cream bar, the moment you have started opening the wrapper, enjoy it like it is the only one you will ever have and don't feel guilty about it afterward. There is no purpose for guilt. If you know you should not have the ice cream bar and your health is important enough to you, you will not have it. If you have decided the enjoyment of the bar is worth it, enjoy the ice cream bar.

When you are living in an enlightened state it is not that you don't enjoy pleasures of the flesh, you are just less likely to make these things your aim.

Dying in every moment is not an excuse to act impulsively but rather an opportunity to really live with a true awareness that our time spent here, in this form, is finite. It will come to an end. So, why fight the end?

Live your life now and prepare for the possibility that you might live to see tomorrow. There are no guarantees.

Occasionally, when I get sick or stressed, I get cold sores on my lip. I can often feel them coming a day or two before they show up and I take Lysine Tablets and put on a Lysine Lip Balm to combat them. For anyone that has ever had a cold sore, they are uncomfortable, quite visually unappealing, and take a few days to go away.

A few months ago I felt a cold sore start to come in under the surface of my lip and I thought "I should take a Lysine Tablet just in case I am alive tomorrow." We do not have to fixate on tomorrow or worry about what will happen when we get there. We must only make some preparations for "just in case I am alive tomorrow" and then continue on with our lives.

If you were to die tonight, how would you live today differently? This meditation is to think on death in a realistic way that affirms life. Not to go checking items off of an extravagant bucket list. This way we can enjoy this life and live it aware of how precious it is. *Die before you die* gives us the freedom to question; is this how I want to live?

In the West we are terrified of death and so we cast it out. We tuck away the dying as far from us as possible and do everything we can to avoid thinking about death and because of this we deny ourselves the lessons that come from associating with the dying. Living in fear of death is death. The second we embrace death, as a part of life, is the second we take our first breath as a living, loving, ascended human being.

This is not to say we should go running to death, or give up when fighting an illness, but rather live your life without the fear of dying because you have already thought on it so clearly that it no longer bothers you. A lot of people are thinking, *David, I'm not ready to die!* I'm not particularly ready to die either. I just know that life will go on, for everyone, including myself and I am incredibly curious as to what is waiting for me on the next plain.

We get lost in our bodies and minds and become their prisoners instead of letting them be our vehicle for movement and free thought. We identify with pain and trauma instead of finding the lessons in the source. Stop fighting your pain and trauma. Embrace it and acknowledge it for what it is, an opportunity.

In the book *Outwitting The Devil* Napoleon Hill interviews the Devil in a *Question and Answer* session and it is one of the most profound books I have ever read. Napoleon asks the Devil "Is failure ever a benefit to man?" The Devil responds;

> *"Yes (…) But few people know that every adversity brings with it the seed of an equivalent advantage."*

We must, at times, look beyond our own lives to find the *equivalent advantage* and remember we are one entity experiencing itself. Where is the benefit to experiencing death, pain, and trauma?

The Devil expands;

> *"I hate to tell you this, but failure often serves as a blessing in disguise because it breaks the grip of hypnotic rhythm and frees the mind for a fresh start."*

I'm incredibly grateful for all of my failures. They have shifted me away from so much of what was not me and back towards what I am. Even if I had to take a fall to snap out of the slumber and realize I was asleep.

Pain is a gift. It is an opportunity to rise above the body. To ascend above this meat and flesh that ails us and be inspired by the way life continues. My body is not a cage. It is my vehicle. The pain is a reminder that this is temporary and I only get to experience this for so long. I am so grateful for all of the moments of pain, they are incredibly *life affirming*. The pain gives me an opportunity to rise above myself and the reactions stirring in my mind as a result of the pain.

If I lived my entire life with no pain, physical or emotional, I wouldn't be the same human being I am today. I would have continued to rely on my body to provide the manual labor necessary to give me a decent income while neglecting my mind as a credible and valuable tool for forward motion.

Every trauma I have experienced showed me something about the pain of the world that connects me deeper to it. It doesn't remove me from the soul of humanity to have experienced trauma! It connects me to its essence and gives me the opportunity to ascend, to be better, and to help others around me do the same.

Why do we have such an issue with pain, evil, and trauma? Accept them gift wrapped. We don't learn much from our moments of comfort and entertainment. Life is experienced in the trenches. Very little is picked up from the sidelines. Did you expect it to be comfortable down here? How incredibly boring would that be?

I live with chronic pain. I don't have to elaborate further. I have watched people die from cancer, childhood leukemia, at war, and slowly inside until they took their own lives. I'm grateful that each of these people lived and each of them showed me something about life. Their lives were not meaningless, no matter how short. The shortest of lives somehow manage to have the greatest of impacts.

Tell a woman that only held her child for a few weeks that love can be only be quantified and weighed out with time and she will tell you that you have a thing or two to learn about love.

Tell me that the child experienced nothing but tragedy in its short existence on this planet and I will tell you the meaning of the child's life is not yours to take. The infant's experience was not yours. To have incubated was to exist, to be loved, to be born, to be held in the palms of something so great that loves you so truly and innocently.

When we grasp at strings and claw at our eyes and ears while screaming to the heavens *"why"* take a moment to understand why you are in so much pain. You have experienced the inverse. What a beautiful gift to have loved and what a tremendously heavy gift to outlive the ones we love. To memorialize them, take lessons from their lives, place them in the sacred vaults of our memories, carrying on the torch of the light of the goodness they carried.

When you start to awake it is a dangerous time because everything can start to appear fake or plastic. It will start to feel like everyone is having the same meaningless conversations and you are alone on this planet. By seeing the plastic existence presented on social media and entertainment, we can start to dissociate from life and begin to think it is meaningless and everyone as stupid, fake, and/or oblivious. You are having what Alan Watts calls the *inverted mystical experience*. It may be a step towards where you are headed but it is not the goal.

Some people get lost in nihilism, existentialism, and absurdism during these times and never find their way out. It's very *punk-rock* to think of life as devoid of any real meaning and with no creator, or a creator that can't tell their elbow from their chin, and we are all alone to figure it out for ourselves. Just us and our over-inflated egos. Between the two of us, we got it. Until we don't.

Nihilism and *existentialism* have very sexy and intelligent followers and they go a long way back. All pain-laden and punk-rock throughout history. They had it the worst, they have it the worst, and you wouldn't believe how bad they have had it. They are also way too stoic and punk-rock to tell you about it, until they tell you about it.

To the mystic the world seems magical. We believe that all human beings have the capacity for goodness. We choose to hope against hope that life is not meaningless. We have faith that humanity's brightest days are ahead while having the awareness that we must work towards them through the service of others to see them. We see that we are all connected through one-consciousness experiencing itself. Why would I not have faith in humanity if they are a part of me? I choose to have faith in myself, this world, this consciousness.

The *nihilist* continues to judge each person they come into contact with for the sins of the world while the *tragic optimist* continues to manifest the love in their hearts into the world around them and, on their journeys, will see others doing the same in some capacity or another. The lens of perspective colors the world we live in and then helps us to paint it for others.

Instead of judging each person I come into contact with for the pain they are carrying, and acting out, I would rather help that person to heal. In beating them there will be no lessons for either of us. In destruction no lessons are ever learned again. And, of course, avoidance has never solved anything. Not all people will be capable of, or interested in, healing.

We can always look for the people operating in the darkness, and thriving, as a reason for *meaninglessness*. The religious man might speak of the punishment that is coming and others may say "lean on karma" and hope they get what is coming to them. These people operating in the darkness, walking in the shade, living in fear, are already living in hell. Why would I wish anything but healing for them?

Adolf Hitler didn't find hell in the end, alone, when he committed suicide. He lived hell in every moment of his existence. He lived fearful, warful, and wrathful. He caused chaos and terror and lived there himself. He inflated his ego, painted his mask, and set out to be the solution to the world's problems by eradicating entire classes and races of people. The complete domination of an egoic and fearful existence left unchecked.

Zen is not a choice to avoid men like this, nor to pretend they do not exist, but to be aware that people like this exist and commit to your own personal choice to do what is right beyond your beating heart by detaching from it. Choosing love is choosing life even if that life is not your own.

You cannot live life on your knees. It is impossible to be a loving coward. The coward lives in fear, is cloaked in it, and acts with fear in the driver seat while love sits in the passenger seat getting screamed at, talked at, or silenced.

If we only focus on the ugliness of war, and never look to learn the lessons, we will find more of it. If the world read more books by the people that lived through the terrors, and less by the ones that caused them while being safely removed, we may even find the mindset that causes war completely unnecessary.

When it comes to war, life, leadership, family, meaning, and beauty I will consult books by Dr. Viktor Frankl and the diary of a little girl who was on the receiving end of the terrors of war in Anne Frank, or the men that were held as prisoners of war in Vietnam and lost years of their lives to torture and insufferable inhumanities to come out better men on the other end.

It is by living through war, not causing it, that one may come to understand it. The same can be said of life. You do not suddenly understand life, or become more wise, because you become a parent. Why is it that a person can find themselves while incarcerated in prison, a man can find himself as a POW, or in a foxhole, or in a ghetto, but the man with an unlimited traveling budget only finds himself on his death bed?

Men are now dying while in line to get to the highest point in the world to satisfy their bucket list. People are traveling halfway across the world to take ayahuasca to achieve the sort of cleansing that already lies within the confines of their own minds. It is no wonder we are spiritually adrift; we are mentally and physically adrift.

We think enlightenment, healing, and success is something that must be quested for. Then when we arrive and take the ayahuasca, touch the highest point of the world, or make a million dollars, we are surprised when we feel, more or less, the same.

Take better journeys and it will be much harder to be disappointed in the outcome because you will keep going. You may even realize there is no finish line. No outcome. Satisfaction can be found at every stop, in every breath, and in every motion between here and there while taking nothing away from the ultimate journey. If we quest for peace and only get halfway there what a wonderful journey we will have been on!

A machine-gunner questing for peace may seem absurd to you. Martin Luther King Jr. was born in 1929 in Atlanta, Georgia into a segregated south. He knew he was a vehicle for peace, even if those around him threw their hands up, or clenched their fists, he kept his arms interlocked with others and his head up. Anne Frank was born of Jewish descent in Germany in 1929, the year Hitler would rise to power. She was born into tragedy and yet remained optimistic and hopeful.

> *"It's really a wonder that I haven't dropped all my ideals, because they seem so absurd and impossible to carry out. Yet I keep them, because in spite of everything, I still believe that people are really good at heart." -*
> *Anne Frank*

In Dr. Viktor Frankl's book *Man's Search for Meaning* he recalls a secondhand story of *The Butcher of Auschwitz,* who committed terrible acts against humanity. *The Butcher* goes onto live out his days and be thought of as a "good guy" by those around him. Destruction of an entire person prevents any further healing for anyone.

If these three, whom have had everything taken from them, not by evil, but by complacency, can believe men are good who am I to say otherwise? Whose sins against me are so great that I cannot forgive them without their permission?

It is not in spite of experiencing war that I quest for peace. It is because I have experienced war that I realize it solves very little and yet we emulate combat in our businesses, our lives, and even in our body language. A lot of us have heard the businessman talking about the new piece of tech or new marketing piece that is going to "wipe out the competition". How to *destroy*, *blow everyone out*, and *win at all costs*.

Alan Watts gives a speech entitled *Die Before You Actually Die* which can be found on YouTube. In it he says;

> *"See when we get the ultimate weapon, with which we know we can be safe because nobody else has it, just because we wanted to get that ultimate safety, and get that ultimate weapon to defeat our enemies it will be suicide because life really is, not the avoidance of death, death is the avoidance of death. The constant terror of death, the constant putting it*

> *off, constant vigilance that one will not die, that is death. What we call life is the fundamental willingness to die."*

This is true in business as well as in life. Some people have tasted business death and no longer fear it. Others have taken a peak at the edge and have been driven mad by it. They live in the fear of business death. They are plagued by it. They fear losing employees, they fear the market shifting, they even fear new opportunities. This is death.

You cannot beat fear with more fear. The person who withdraws from the world to avoid being hurt only hurts. The person who attacks first because they have been attacked, lives in pain. There is no love to be found there. There is a better way.

> *"Darkness cannot drive out darkness; only light can do that. Hate cannot drive out hate; only love can do that."*
> Dr. Martin Luther King, Jr.

We must live for love. I'm not talking about romantic love. Money and security are not a viable alternative for love. If you don't find any love in your life it is no wonder you have considered pressing the reset button. In most ordinary situations, you must give love to receive it. Love something. Be passionate about something.

The reason people give up is they have found they are no longer in a *workable game*. They are either set up to lose, or set up to win, and the game becomes boring. This is the reason that both players will tend to give up on a chess game when they realize they are few moves out from a check mate. There is no reason to play these moves out. Unfortunately this is the same reason many people commit suicide. They have lost hope of anything different and exciting. They are stuck in autopilot and they are terrified of change.

      Human beings enjoy a good gamble! We like the concept of a little risk and a little luck, meeting with some skill and possibly having the opportunity to change our stars. This is what Alan Watts calls a "workable game"; an optimal combination of skill and chance. Games of pure chance are boring and one can be encouraged to cheat a little to introduce some skill. Games of pure skill can become exhausting and there is very little room for play.

      A lot of people assume that gambling is a bad thing. They would be right if we continued to play the *slot machines of life* dropping in our time and pulling the handle and hoping for pure chance to come and rescue us. Too many people kill themselves instead of leaving the table for one where they can utilize their skill and find a more workable game.

      The inverse of this is sitting at a table where you have *gamed the game*. You're counting cards, you've got it all figured out, and now you must just keep your foot on the gas pedal until you bleed the house. This is equally as boring. An optimal game must involve risk. Taking the risk out of a game doesn't make it enjoyable.

You must find a game you enjoy and therefore there must be an element of risk or life becomes boring. Alan Watts goes on in the same speech;

> *"The gamble has to rest on the assumption that this game is superb. No other assumption will work. The universe is meant to be trusted. This is the basis for all gambling."*

If you find you want to clear the board and start over, clear the board. Play a different game. There may be people around you, bosses, friends, family, co-workers telling you that you must continue to play the hand you are dealt. There is no law against walking away from a game that does not serve you. There will be people who say "there ought to be a law against it" who live fear-based and controlling lives. They love contracts, commitments, and control.

Fear based, controlling people do not enable us to live our best lives. They make it impossible for us to act. They do not live with faith. They don't believe the game is superb. They believe it is flawed and live terrified while seeking to control the game and manipulate its players. We all have one of these bastards living inside of us. It is our *self-conscious questioner* constantly doubting us and getting in our way. This voice may live outside of us, as well, but we carry it with us. Who told you these lies about yourself and why do you continue to do it for them?

This is the *self-conscious person* living within you, holding you back. Spend less time policing yourself, and more time feeling free to live and die in each moment. If you have lived your entire life trying to control each moment suddenly realizing it is okay to die is incredibly freeing. What *must* be accomplished before we die? What *must* we do? The answer is nothing.

Now, you can either decide to go kill yourself now or you can live your life feeling incredibly free to live as you see fit! You do not have to live. Your children will be okay, eventually. The world will keep spinning. Death is a part of life. Will you cause pain to other people? Sure! That does not obligate you to stay here.

When we feel obligated to this world it takes the fun out of it! It's like a mandatory fun day at work. Is it possible to have fun when it is mandatory? Yes. It just isn't easy because the entire time you are there, you are there knowing you have to be. You feel obligated. You are stuck.

People who feel obligated to their work typically feel obligated to their children. They let their children know it, too! They say "I do this for you. I work so I can put a roof over your head." They begin to think of *love* as *self-sacrifice*. Going to work and doing something you hate so your children can eat. "I sacrificed everything for my kids". Well, how noble. How did that work out for you? How is it working out for them?

You must first *want to do something* to ever hope to experience joy while participating in it. Whether this is building homes, building a business, or simply learning how to play the guitar. If you should ever hope to go into a state of Mushin during these activities and experience the peace of no mind while performing a task in mastery, you will have to spend time working or practicing on it. You must want to be there.

The want should be your own. This is the difference between taking a child to piano lessons because you feel it is the next necessary step in the child's development and the child asking to play piano and then having difficulty pulling them away from the piano at dinner time.

People get stuck in *whys* and blow them out of proportion to this massive driving life goal that will keep us going in our darkest hours. The problem for most people's stupid whys is they have never considered the person considering them. For example; if your why is your kids your why sucks.

How could a child feel free to live their lives for themselves when their parents live for them? How burdensome. There is a difference between giving to your child because you experience deep joy from giving to them and sacrificing yourself, painfully, for them to witness. What is the best possible outcome? Isn't that a heavy burden for them to shoulder? We do the same thing in our businesses.

So many parents claim to lose themselves in their children but what they are really doing is preventing their children from getting lost in themselves. Let go of your mini-me, let go of your child, and allow them to live their lives. Do not take ownership of their lives, only your role in their journey. For many of you this is a terrifying thought. It forces the burden of living back on you! Now, to shatter the old misconceptions and not look at life as a burden.

If we see life as *the gift of the present moment* we will only see a life worth living. It is only by attaching to the moments around the present moment that life suddenly feels burdensome. If we can die in each moment, we can live freely in each moment, and we will naturally teach our children to do the same.

I took my nephew and my son for a bike ride the other day to and from school. My nephew had never made the trek with us before and so this was a new experience for him. He got the most joy out of saying "good morning" and "good afternoon" to those we passed than any other part of our adventure. He exclaimed how much *he loved to say "good morning" to people* and that *he would remember this day forever*.

He was not worried about the conversation he would have with these random people we came across nor if we would ever see them again. He simply said "good morning" because it felt good for him to say it as he whizzed passed on his bike, and he did not get caught up on whether or not people said it back.

We should live our lives more like a child on a bike. We can say "good morning" to the people we pass, notice the blue skies, we can get scared about cars whizzing by, we can take a peek at the dead crow on the sidewalk, but let's keep going. If you don't like the direction, take a detour, or shift paths entirely. We need not take it more seriously than this to enjoy our lives. We are a kid, on a bike, with a day to spend. How will we spend it?

My nephew brought up the dead crow as we passed. "Aw, that's sad" he said. "Why?" I asked him. "Because he's dead." "Do you think he's still there?" I hollered back. "Would you still think it was sad if you realized he's still alive somewhere? Maybe he's an eagle now. Would it still be sad?" "No." He said. "It would be awesome!" I told him, as we rolled on by on our bikes, *"that's kind of how life works. It never stops."*

The alternative to that is the highly self-conscious and fearful adults manifesting, surrounding, and shaping the world we live in. Alan Watts, once again, leads us home by painting a clear picture of the self-conscious state of mind manifested.

> *"A community of people which is always watching itself, through its agents. So that, you know, in a Nazi state they're not only the ordinary policeman on the beat but there's a block captain for every area and there's some kind of a sneak or traitor who is going to inform the authorities everywhere hidden."*

> *"This community is watching itself all the time because it's a community which doesn't trust itself. And a*

community which constantly watches itself is like a person who is always watching himself and holding a club over his head to go clunk the minute he might be in danger of doing something wrong(...)"

"If I say now 'my right hand is my main active hand but I don't know whether or not I can trust it. I don't know what it's going to do. So I've got to keep control of it with my left hand.' So, always the left hand is controlling the right hand... See? I've lost a hand by doing that."

"So, in exactly the same way when any community of people is founded on mutual mistrust it sort of loses half of itself (...)"

"So the basis of any community, and thus the basis of any game, is the act of faith that I will gamble. I will bet my life on this seed. You see, that is also fundamentally not only the attitude of faith but it is the attitude of love. Love is self-giving."

Love is *self-giving*. Not *self-sacrificing*. There is an important distinction to make. The same speaker who delivered the *color exercise* I told you about earlier, also told us that she gives from her saucer, not from her cup, and teaches her children to do the same. In order to do this, she wakes up at 4:45am every day to fill her cup so much that it spills over.

With the left hand watching the right hand both hands are incapable of true movement because they are not able to move without the other. This is the opposite of faith, the opposite of love. This is the foundation for our political structure, our businesses, many marriages, friendships, relationships between parents and children, and even the relationship we have with ourselves.

Laws against cheating do not enforce love. Contracts do not enforce loyalty. Taking vows of commitment in our youths to carry through into our adulthood work as well as employees signing long-term contracts with no exit strategy in their youth. Love is a letting go of direct control. It is faith in yourself, another person, and the world around you.

Love is not self-sacrificing. You are giving yourself to your business, your children, and the world because they are connected to you. In fact, they *are* you. We will get into that more in the final chapter, *Nirvana & Bodhi*.

In Bodhicitta, you find yourself in the altruistic service of others above yourself. You have realized the inner-connectedness of everything, and wish to serve the greater being, bringing it further into healing and harmony. As Alan Watts puts it, "You as God, are constantly giving yourself away to you." Giving of yourself is divine love.

Live every moment as if it is the last time you will do it. It is. You may do similar things at other times but you will never have this moment again. No picture, no video, no personal diary can encapsulate a moment perfectly and hold it in time. You can only experience it once.

When we understand we truly only get to do this once we don't feel obligated to have fun or do the things we have always wanted to do, or see the things we have always wanted to see. We are grateful to wake up, once again, to another day. We recognize "we only get to do this once" does not mean "we only get to live this life once" it means "*this*" as in "this, particular moment". You will only read this sentence for a first time once, and yet you may read it again, but never again for the first time. That is the opportunity we get in every moment.

If we treated each greeting as if we were dead only a few moments ago, and this moment was not possible, how grateful we will be to see humanity in this form again. How happy we will be to see an old friend, our children, or our spouse returning home. How wonderful to wake up in the middle of the night and still have these people in this house. How wonderful to have our co-workers, our spiritual practice, the sunlight, another day, another opportunity! What a gift! Just moments ago I thought I should not ever see any of this again and yet here I am *living again*. What a fortunate human being I am to have died and lived again and see with these eyes what I can see.

> *"Live as if you were living for the second time and had acted as wrongly the first time as you are about to act now." -Napoleon Hill*

    This time live it. This time see it. This time experience it with your own eyes, ears, and hands. As ee cummings writes "now the ears of my ears awake and now the eyes of my eyes are opened". How beautiful music is when we understand its purposelessness. How tremendous this dance of life, and how fortunate we the dancers.

    Helen Keller, who was born deaf and blind, asked a friend what she saw during a walk in the woods. Her friend responded "nothing of note." She was inspired to write an essay entitled *Three Days to See*.

> *"I wondered how it was possible to walk for an hour through the woods and see 'nothing of note'. I who cannot see find hundreds of things: the delicate symmetry of a leaf, the smooth skin of a silver birch, the rough, shaggy bark of a pine... use your eyes as if tomorrow you will have been stricken blind." -Helen Keller*

    How wonderful to have seen the stars in this lifetime. How sacred they would be to us if we never saw them again. If tonight, for some reason the stars were no longer visible to us, how fondly we would remember them. Isn't it interesting that we are, quite literally, stardust? What star must disappear from your night sky for you to appreciate it? How wonderful it is to be able to see these things! What a gift to be able to behold them. To be able to see beauty in other people. To see beauty in yourself before the stars fade into the night sky.

> *"If the stars should appear one night in a thousand years, how would men believe and adore; and preserve for many generations the remembrance of the city of God which had been shown! But every night come out these envoys of beauty, and light the universe with their admonishing smile."— Ralph Waldo Emerson, Nature and Selected Essays*

Just to not take ourselves too seriously, let's visit Calvin as he sits under the stars, propped up with his hands behind him and his stuffed tiger and best friend Hobbes by his side.

> *"If people sat outside and looked at the stars each night, I'll bet they'd live a lot differently."*

If your only meditation was to sit under the stars every night, you will have lived a life well reflected on. We don't sit under the stars to make sense of them but to admire their beauty from afar. There is nothing more purposeless than gazing at the stars but many things equally as purposeless. What beautiful stars burn so brightly before me every day shuffling before my feet! These tiny beauties. I am so fortunate to be a father. How fortunate I am, when I am capable, to truly see every person before me.

    Our job is to not stretch ourselves so thin, in every capacity that we control everything, making everyone an extension of ourselves. Our job is to provide space for other people to walk into. How can we do this if we are always busy? Look at the stars, play guitar, find yourself lost in play at work. Live your life as a child on a bike saying "good morning" to each person you pass, and let the ego die in each moment.

    Make your why so big that you may not get there in this lifetime. This will challenge you to think bigger, include more people, and set the foundation for fundamental change. If our why is big enough, and set up on a firm foundation, with enough people involved, the mission will outlive us.

    For those of you that are business owners, you know what this means; creating and establishing systems that will help your mission to succeed whether or not your heart continues to beat. The mission must outlive me. The mission is critical. What is the mission?

    I have many missions in life and all of them must continue past my exit of this world. We will tackle a few of them now; I want my family to continue to eat, I want the world to become more peaceful, and I want people to realize they are enough.

Family to eat: Many of us want our families to continue to eat passed our exit from this world. Some of us have children that have graduated, and they will be okay, others have young children who are financially dependent on us setting up systems to sustain them if we should die.

The first thing to realize is that your children will continue to be okay even if you were to die tomorrow. Logically play it out in your mind and understand they will continue to sustain the nourishment they need for their survival.

The goal is to continue to improve or sustain their situation in the event of your departure. In order to do this, the income must continue to be received after we exit. This is possible through a) hoarding money b) having ownership in a company, stock, real estate, or platform which will continue to yield or exist after your death or c) having some sort of lump sum death gratuity which will pay out, and hopefully sustain your family until they no longer need sustainment.

More Peaceful World: I write books and have interviewed people on podcasts so that the knowledge I have been fortunate enough to come across in my travels can be passed onto others.

My goal is that each of my books have an idea, a concept, or a thought that is worth reading even if I am no longer here. Whether that is for one person, one-hundred thousand, or for one of my children, is not completely up to me.

Self-Realization of Enough: to awaken other people is the single, most important goal of my life. If you are awake, you are less apt to give way to drifting, or hopelessness, and will continue to move forward. Even if that means leaving a piece of you behind that no longer serves your best interest, like we discussed earlier in this book.

I am enough. There is enough. That will be enough. Once you realize these things, everything else is the bonus round.

In the book *Lessons from the Hanois Hilton* the authors showcases James Stockdale's *From the 30,000-Foot Level: Three Elements of a Sustainable Culture.* James was one of the *Senior Ranking Officers* in, what was referred to as, the Hanois Hilton, a prisoner of war camp in Vietnam. He established these elements so that the mission could continue in the event of his/or anyone else's death.

In order to have a *mission that outlives us* we cannot act alone. If you have always been a lone-wolf you may want to learn to play nice with others and find yourself a wolf pack or several. The ego often believes it has the answer. You cannot continue to accomplish passed the grave unless you have hired.

The *Three Elements of a Sustainable Culture* are virtual leadership, viral culture, and social network.

Virtual Leadership; establish a mission, a credo, rules for the road, and daily practices without presence.

Viral Culture; instead of competing for morsels and setting individual goals, focus on high-performance squad goals to travel towards as a team.

Social Network; inclusive communication and setting the expectation that each would do what they could when they could.

These rules were founded in a prisoner of war camp decades before the internet existed and yet we have very modern words being used; "virtual", "viral", and "social network". You have much more accessibility to a person half the world away than John Stockdale had to his comrades that were just a few feet from his cell. Meanwhile, others were being held on the other side of the country, in a different POW camp altogether, and he was still able to have a tremendous amount of influence over these men.

There has never been a better time in history to start a business, work in real estate, or join a multi-level marketing platform. Multi-level marketing mixed with altruism creates opportunities for servant leadership, new business opportunities, and chances for incentivized servant leadership.

Massive amounts of money are being redistributed and governments and big businesses have less control over it than ever. It is becoming harder and harder to predict how this economy will change over the years. This is why it is so important to continue to trust your intuition and participate in the world economy.

The world is terrified. Especially the powers that be. Power and financial opportunities are shifting and becoming harder and harder to regulate. How wonderful! Jeff Bezos left his job as a *Senior-Vice President* of an investment firm to start an online bookselling company in his garage in 1995. 24 years later and Amazon is a powerhouse and Jeff Bezos is the richest man in the world.

There are so many opportunities for death and rebirth in the modern business world and yet we live paralyzed by fear of failure. Play the game. Trust your intuition. Live and die in every moment. What is failure other than another chance to live again?

10. Nirvana & Bodhi

There were times I thought about making this final chapter its own book. It developed a life of its own. All of these world religions support the same thought; God is within us. Yet, we feel so far removed from God. In this life, there are those amongst us, who have ascended the flesh. We recognize few of them because it is not their goal to gain recognition.

In this final chapter we add the Christian, Hindu, Muslim, and Jewish faiths into the mix alongside new age mysticism and analyze ascension or Nirvana. The literal sigh of relief and what comes next. Do we stay in this altered state of ascended consciousnesses, *Nirvana*, or do we forego this state to serve mankind and all other sentient beings in the state of *Bodhi*? Do we have a choice, or are we pawns on a chessboard acting out the moves of some higher-power? All of these questions are worth analyzing in this final step we are taking together in this book.

I sincerely hope that you have enjoyed reading this book as much as I have enjoyed writing it. It truly has been a pleasure and I am grateful that you have chosen to take this journey with me. It is my hope that you have read this book in order and this is the last chapter you will read, though I know many of you will skip to the end and I am okay with this as well.

The last step in this journey, with this book, is to express the connectivity of everything and I will do this with the help of many well-recognized world religions. If your religion is not mentioned, while others, like Christianity are mentioned several times, please do not take offense. Christianity is the Religion of the West. There is nothing wrong with this, it is simply the truth.

    I do not choose any one religion or *practice* as right but find the light study of all them interesting. Some might call this Baha'i, others may call this Hinduism, some may say I practice Zen, or that I am a mystic. I have had others argue with me that I am a Christian and tell me they have caught me preaching. Others have encouraged me to look into the mystical side of Islam, which is Sufism. I am grateful for every comparison, encouragement, and accusation!

    I have called myself many things in the past as well. Not all of them true. It has been a long journey to healing and I tell people "I came across Zen because the alternative was going crazy". I enjoy the practice. I identify with the culture, the people, and the literature around it. I don't hold it more highly than other religions or practices but I find the text more consistent and the people delivering the message colorful and entertaining. I never believed life was little or insignificant.

    I never believed I was supposed to spend my life on my knees. I have my own attachments to what religion is, and is not, and I am working to overcome them. You see, I tend to enjoy deeply spiritual people of all religions while having a particular disdain for any religious person, like I would a government bureaucrat, claiming to have, or to be, the answer. Much of what has become Christianity more closely resembles consumerism and I believe Jesus would be more likely to bring a bullwhip to many of these churches than he would be to receive communion at one of them.

I love and enjoy the teachings of Jesus. Some of them, I believe, have been manipulated or misconstrued and I don't claim to be the answer to decipher their meanings. I just know that anything written, and considered dead, leaves itself open to manipulation or misinterpretation by man over time. This is only natural. I don't believe, by any stretch of the imagination, that Christianity is the only religion that has been hijacked by the religious. You can point to anyone of them, but here we are in the West.

I also acknowledge the goodness Christians do, and have done, over time while not disregarding the atrocities that can only be attributed to truly believing you have an answer and someone must understand your answer, in order for their salvation. One would go to great lengths to bring about salvation to an ignorant person if they thought the well-being of their eternal soul might depend on it.

Religion also has a way of being conveniently politically aligned. When money is what we worship we cannot worship it without the permission of Caesar. Caesar, the state, has replaced God. So, we seek to use the state to control others into salvation. Control is not love and was never the mission.

I have a deep love for Jesus the Savage. The Barbarian with the superior and sharpened intellect who took time to tell stories to children. Who took time to listen and to grasp. The man who took time to intervene in the lives of prostitutes and washed the feet of lepers. We took so much away from him by removing him from *humanity*.

I love all of these religious rebels who challenged the authorities of their time. The history books are long with people who have stood up to the establishment. They would be even longer but the victor writes the books the captives are allowed to distribute. A lot of wisdom has survived but we must take everything for what it is and then look deeper.

This last chapter will challenge you, your beliefs, your thoughts about humanity, and hopefully your thoughts about you. I am about to make a claim and I am not the first one to say it but it could not be said loudly at any other time throughout history without being burned at the stake for it.

There is an awakening coming and the message has been said in parables before by wise people that knew their audience. Every person you meet is part of the all existing consciousness, we are healing or hurting ourselves. If God has created us all in "his" image, every face you look into is the face of god, including your own.

Genesis 1:27

"(27) So God created man in His own image; in the image of God He created him; male and female He created them."

He created them in his own image. We are created of mud. We are quite literally stardust shaped into the Image of God. Yet, we speak so poorly about ourselves and one another. Casting judgement and creating hell on earth manifested here for us to live out every day. Why do we insist on these things? We have decided we are weak, powerless, and that we must live to control others, for others must be feared because they are not of us. How could someone be trusted to look after themselves? After all, salvation is something *we* have figured out. *They* just need to understand it.

It is easy to think about God, business, religion, relationships, parenting, all as, essentially, one thing. This is because it is. This is the genius in the parable. Many of the greatest teachers, prophets, and shamans spoke in parables, telling stories people could understand and then apply to everything, as one thing. This is why we all have a great, deep love, for a children's story told in parables. I am so attached to these stories I have two of them written on my arms as a visual reminder.

The Giving Tree by Shel Silverstein, who was drafted into the Army during the Korean War, is one of the most perfect children's stories ever told. So many analogies and connections can be made. The story is about a boy and a tree who grow old together. The tree is constantly giving of herself to the boy. The boy goes off and comes back with new requests. In the end, they finish their time quietly sitting together, resting happily, an old man and a stump of a tree.

The goal is to love all people the same regardless of their stage of enlightenment or current use to you in your life. When we start seeing people as a means to an end, or a transaction, we lose our spiritual connection to humanity. Without a connection to humanity we lose connection to ourselves.

To love the acorn just as much as the oak tree is important. The acorn has all the potential of the oak tree within a tiny seed. The entire life force of everything it needs composed within the DNA of the acorn then merges with and is sustained by the world. Someday when the tree gives way to rot and is consumed by termites, it will fall to the floor and be covered in moss, or fungus, and new life will have an opportunity to grow.

We should love the child as much as the adult, the adult as much as the elderly, and the elderly as much as the senile. We are all one experiencing entity. The moment we start to discard one another we discard ourselves.

To bring this back to business. I have never made the change during my real estate career to abandon my price-point for working in the luxury market. People have pushed me there, told me they would pay for my marketing and would mentor me but I have no interest in leaving behind my people for a higher paycheck. I make enough money and value the person at $200,000 as much as the person at $2,000,000.

Another constant suggestion in real estate is only working with listings or the transition from working with buyers. We constantly talk about *opportunity costs* but rarely consider the toll it takes on our soul to tell people they can't afford to work with us.

Some people subsidize their businesses with volunteer work, or by donating large sums of money, to help them feel balanced by the lack of integrity they conduct themselves with while wearing their business hats. I still volunteer but I also don't make delineations on who I can and cannot help when they walk into my office or my open house. If they have a beating heart I can help them.

Everyone needs something. In the real estate industry this could be a fellow agent, a renter, a buyer, or a "nosey" neighbor. The second you stop trying to decide who is worth your time is the moment you will open doors on the *spiritual practice* that you are currently calling a "business".

My mom and my dad always had a soft spot for homeless people. I have witnessed my dad stop, several times throughout my life, when he sees a homeless person and walk into a grocery store to buy a few meals and some hot food and then race out to find them. Then he would walk over and hand it to them, give them the money he had in his wallet, and he would do something I have never watched anyone do since; he would spend time with them.

As a child, watching my dad give his time to people in this way was always one of the most peculiar and interesting things about my dad. He never had much money but he would give what he could to who he could, when he could. My dad spent time homeless. He finished high school homeless and met my mom.

My mom can't drive by a person who is in pain without saying "that's somebody's child". Throughout my life I have witnessed my mom over-extend herself to help strangers. Recently, she picked up a mentally-ill young lady and brought her into her home to get clean, eat some food, stay the night, and call her family. She just as quickly threw herself into a gang-fight to break it up a few years back in front of a Target. She makes me nervous but life was never meant to be safe.

We seek safety and security and instead find death. We wonder why we are bored. We have made money our God and have built walls up, to keep ourselves out. We are the corner office. We are the top floor. We are the ones with the awards mounted on our walls. We are the better ones. People are numbers, transactions, and deals and we wonder why we feel lifeless.

We don't have to close our businesses, sell everything we own, and then head off to combat human-trafficking first-hand to feel of service. Though, if you feel compelled to do so, I will not tell you "no". We must only serve the person in front of us. Give of ourselves and our time.

We have all had the experience where the *spiritual-practitioner* in front of us makes us feel seen, heard, and validated. Whether that is the *barista* that takes extra time to inquire about your day, your drink, or where you are headed or the CPA that reviews your taxes as if they were their own. Service is important and we have forgotten that as a society. We have exchanged service for convenience because convenience means "more". More of what? What do you need more of? How could you not attain that through service?

Some people serve others by creating amazing opportunities and systems and make a significant amount of money by doing so and help others do the same. Fantastic! Just don't forget who is serving you, and remember to serve them.

No person is a means to an end. No person is a transaction. No agent must close a certain number of deals to be considered worthy. When we let people know they are not worthy of our time we let ourselves know we are unworthy as well. Who told you this? Why are you telling other people the same thing? Who are you not worthy of? Why pass that pain on?

Every person is connected to you and you are connected to every person. In every person you should see Christ, The Face of The Buddha, Allah, or yourself. The scripture is there to support this from all major religions. We know this inherently to be true. If every person is God, an image of God, or has God within them, why do we stop short of saying "God is within me" and then feel worthy?

Dick Gregory, a free-thinking activist and comedian who was drafted during the Vietnam War, was asked during an interview he gave towards the end of his life if he fasts because he feels it brings him closer to God. He taps his chest and says; "I'm God. You're

God." We'll get to the rest of his answer later but let's stop there for a moment. I believe he is right. However, if we had said this at any other time throughout history, we would have been burned for heresy, or at the very least publicly discredited. Today if I were to say this out loud to the wrong person, I might be committed, or at the very least medicated.

This was true of many of the prophets in their days. They had to use the words necessary in order to not be stoned, beaten, crucified, or otherwise killed before their time. They took on the religious and political institutions of their day. Many thought they were crazy or called them *heretics*. What should they have done? What would the world look like today if these people had dropped their ideals to become more normal?

What is average? How does the normal person in America behave? Is this what you want to emulate?

> *"According to the A.C. Nielsen Co., the average American watches more than 4 hours of TV each day (or 28 hours/week, or 2 months of nonstop TV-watching per year). In a 65-year life, that person will have spent 9 years glued to the tube." -CSUN.EDU*

> *"Americans check their phone on average once every 12 minutes – burying their heads in their phones 80*

> *times a day, according to new research." -NY Post*

I could not tolerate this sort of insanity! This complacency is disgusting. It keeps us intellectually lazy, entertained, dull and prone to manipulation. So few are coming to their own conclusions about anything. This keeps us debating one another and away from talking, thinking, or exploring new answers.

> *"If a house is divided against itself, it cannot stand." -Mark 3:25*

Fitting into a dysfunctional world does not make us healthy. We throw around a lot of diagnosis to keep ourselves from feeling whole, useful, and purposeful. How could we hope to heal the world if we, ourselves, are broken? So, we identify as ADD, ADHD, Autistic, or Bipolar, and we seek to medicate away the intolerance we feel for a broken, angry, and hurting world. We should not medicate away the anger we feel at the suggestion we cannot be trusted and therefore should be placed in chains. Think of your differences as gifts and learn to utilize them.

I said in my first book, *if you can't help a person's soul, you can't help a person sell*. It's all connected. You can't be a broken, greasy salesman who takes advantage of people and feel spiritually fulfilled at church. You can't feel spiritually fulfilled and hate your job. You can't exercise gratitude by taking. You can be grateful for receiving but you can't be grateful for what you have taken.

As Americans we have a funny way of expressing gratitude. Dick Gregory turned me onto this in a video where he spoke on fasting. He explains that if a boss paid you $1,000 a week and you wanted to do something nice for him, you wouldn't charge him $10,000 for the week, you would work the week for free. On Thanksgiving, a day when we are supposed to be grateful for what we have, we eat more than ever.

I look at Christmas, Thanksgiving, and even Memorial Day in this country and it is obvious that we celebrate everything with consumerism. Very few of us give because we are grateful. Instead we find these times of gratitude to think about the things we don't have and go get them at a discount.

Why in the world is it normal to have a *Memorial Day Sale?* People died at war so save money on appliances and take the day off to barbecue and play in the pool. I don't wish to fit into the world the way it has been presented to me. I know we are better than the foot that is currently forward. I know we are better *now*. Where is the disconnect?

As human beings we preoccupy ourselves with some of the wildest endeavors in the hope that we will someday find immortality. We will game the game. It's exciting to write about but we cannot beat nature. We cannot conquer space. We cannot beat other countries. Nothing will bend to our will. We can only live in harmony with these things or destroy everything. Conquering requires might, love requires courage.

Psychology is becoming the Religion of the West for the irreligious. It keeps us divided, diagnosed, and held captive. Instead of a therapist being like a mechanic that we visit for a tune up during a time of need and then are released back to the road, we have made weekly returns back and have committed ourselves to being broken as long as we continue returning.

Just like religion, there are many sects in psychology. All with their own schools of thought, all tracing back lineage to some brilliant individual who is untouchable. The divine Freud, or one of his apostles, come to look down the brim of their glasses, one step removed from humanity. God forbid, we see with our own eyes the human being standing before us. God forbid we hear them with our ears and guide them with our words for them.

Psychology is holding us captive at this point. We are now in a situation, much like religion, where once a week we are asked to come back, as the little broken birds we are, needing our weekly salvation, and so we turn away from us. We turn away from humanity. It is the premise that we can't trust ourselves. We can't trust our intuition. We are naturally bad, evil, and lazy.

When children realize something is wrong with the world they want to fix it immediately. I take my kids hiking and often, at the foot of the trails, people leave large items of trash instead of taking it to the dump. My kids ask to pick it up and I tell them "no". When children see a person who is hungry, they ask to feed that person. When children see a person sleeping on a street corner they want that person to sleep under a roof. They can't understand the wickedness of the world and the seemingly simple answers to these problems that are denied by adults.

Why does a country with so much money have trouble feeding, housing, and taking care of the people that live here? The answer is simple; we aren't grateful. Grateful people give. Fearful people take. We raise our children to look the other way. We tell them about the people that lost themselves to drugs or made poor decisions but children know human beings don't stop being worthy because they are in pain. As hard as we try to convince them otherwise.

When money is more important than people we will honor money above people. Honor the person, serve humanity through your industry, and the money will likely be a bi-product. This was the secret to my success; I treated everyone as if they were worthy of my time. This doesn't make you crazy, as much as the coaching world will try to tell you otherwise.

I was fresh out of the Marine Corps and service was more important than the obscene amount of money that could be made in this industry. I had no idea the sort of money I would make the next month was even possible. I just knew I could make people feel better about the buying process and themselves than real estate agents had made me feel during the home-buying process. I opened seven escrows in my first month and made over $30,000 in my second and I had fun doing it.

After being turned onto *The Millionaire Real Estate Agent* by Gary Keller by a local successful Realtor who would become a mentor of mine, I recognized a team is ran the same way as an *Infantry Company* in the Marine Corps. The small unit leadership with different squads having squad leaders with different tasks and specialties made sense to me immediately and I began applying that knowledge alongside war-tactics to business.

I set out to serve other agents and turn them onto the information I had obtained and we became force-multipliers. We all hunted together, had high splits, and we were having tons of fun. People from the outside had no idea how we were obtaining success.

I got into coaching and suddenly realized how little I was, how far behind I was, and how much I was doing wrong. I stopped trusting my intuition. I started growing to grow because everyone told me "more is the answer". We set out to win and I lost our way.

When you are the one blazing the trail it is important to be connected to the Oneness, wherever you find it, lest you depend on the fear-based ego to run your business. Love is replaced with control. Having fun is replaced with the fear of doing the wrong things. You realize, for the first time ever, you can fall, while still wanting to climb higher and higher. The ego hates to die and will do anything to stay alive and thriving, on the throne. Stop feeding that ugly bastard.

To step outside of the coaching arena is insanity. Just ask all the coaches, their clients under contract, and all the affiliates making money off of their clients; all those programs and systems that are so incredibly important for your success. If you fail, it is because you didn't perform enough of the *sacraments*. You need to buy more product, you need to do more, salvation is right around the corner. You are on your way! Just don't stop spending money.

Just like how Psychology is the Religion of the West, Coaching is the Religion of the Business World. All different sects of the same church. All with their links back to their own personal, untouchable messiah.

You could become absolutely rich by trusting your intuition. Business can be won by properly serving one community, one family, one person at a time. It is not the coach, the psychologist, or the priest who is responsible to fix you. These descendants and archbishops of the anointed ones themselves.

We all know the person, the agent, the man, the woman, who constantly leaves one team, one broker, one lover, one business at a time, for another one looking to be made whole. All the while resenting the cast of souls behind them that were not up to the task. They are stuck in a perpetual state of searching.

Your first job is to realize you are not broken. You are whole. There is a coaching program out there, and I won't name it by name, but one of the core beliefs is that you are broken. Believing you are broken is the worst of all limiting beliefs. Success in this program starts out by believing you are broken. How could you ever hope to feel good about yourself while accomplishing anything with this mindset? How can we heal the world while believing we are fundamentally flawed?

Do we not work now? Are we not capable now? We always know what the next step is on our journey. We get caught up and lost in making plans. We work now! What is broken now? It takes a lot of responsibility to admit we are not broken. If we admit we are not broken then we have the power to change. We have become a people that goes from person to person asking for their permission to shackle ourselves to them and their ways.

The alternative is that we know what must be done and are simply not doing it. Doesn't that ring a little more true? When you realize, or are willing to accept, that you are whole and need not to quest outward for the missing piece to make you right, or make you whole, it is terrifying and freeing. Now you are responsible for this moment. So many people paint this with a negative light; the thought they are responsible for this moment feels synonymous with failure. Are you not here? Did you not wake up this morning? Instead, be responsible for this moment like you are for your breath, with ease.

Once this newfound responsibility for your own life, experiences, and perspective comes into play it can be very overwhelming and it can also be incredibly freeing. The desire to serve the world is now in you. The desire to replace self-sacrifice with self-giving makes sense. Now, it is time to really find out what our purpose is, right? Not quite. That's where the overwhelming feelings come in. The thought that *now everything must change*. You mustn't change anything.

You must not do anything. That's the point. You have a choice. Whether you are consciously making them, or not, is on you. Everything is a response to your surroundings. Everything is a spiritual practice in the human form. It is beautiful, awful, tragic, and uplifting.

You may not need a career change, you may just need a perspective shift. Just serve the person in front of you. Smile. Give love without expectation of a return and time without the purpose of getting somewhere and you will find your peace.

> *"Never worry about numbers. Help one person at a time and always start with the person nearest you." -Mother Teresa*

Serving another person without taking ownership of their journey is important. Whether someone is an acorn or an oak tree, we love and serve them. I don't believe salvation is external for anyone. This is why I know I am no one's answer. If I believe I was, or knew the answer, I would be put in a rough position. That would make the assumption that I know better for that person than they know for themselves. This is where bosses, team leads, brokers, managers, politicians, and religious leaders lose their way. They stop serving and start controlling because they believe they know better.

    If I believed I knew what was better for you I would do just about anything to help you. At first, I might inspire you. Then I might lead from the front. If that didn't work, I might counsel you. Make sure you understood the reasoning. If you refused to listen to my advice from me I might have someone else approach you who agreed with my viewpoints. If you continued to believe that I didn't know better for you I might coerce, incentivize, or manipulate you. In a last ditch effort for you to see things my way I may threaten to fire you, hoping you might see it my way and seek your salvation before the firing. Faced with your own demise you might see it my way and be successful. If you failed to adapt, I would fire you, then seek to destroy you by covertly or overtly destroying your reputation and encouraging others not to work with you because of one reason or another.

    Business is not so different from life. Business mirrors life in every way possible. It is life. Just as much as children, God, love, and death are life. There is no line in the sand. There is no balance. There are no compartments in which anything must fit into nicely. There is no right way or path to success.

    If you don't fit in today we medicate, we institutionalize, we imprison, and we ostracize. This sort of abandonment by society leaves a person believing they are broken, removed from hope, and removed from rehabilitation. This is what happens when we replace the self with state, religion, politics, coaching, or psychology; we pass off the keys to our own kingdom.

Almost every human being can be diagnosed or labeled as something or other; an over-achiever, under-achiever, hyper-active, a "snowflake". I'm not saying there are not people out there that don't need a little extra help or maybe even to be medicated. I am saying we should take these labels and diagnosis and get to work transcending the body. This would include mentally engaging your own deficiencies and attributes by being aware of them.

My body identifies as autistic. I take the guidebook as an instruction manual for a starting place with my brain and body. By the end of this life I hope to do things with this body comparable to what Jimi-Hendrix could do with a guitar. I desire to break all the rules, transcend limitations, and live my life as a bit of a rascal. It's more fun this way.

For a while I believed I was broken. I found the words to justify this. It wasn't hard. I was supplied with them. When the perspective shifted energy changed like a shifting tide and I was suddenly overwhelmed with information from everywhere and this feeling that I am *whole*. Nothing changed except the perspective.

When the perspective of my mind changed so did the direction of my life. I wish to help others that are *close to suicide*. I want to turn them onto this *die before you die lifestyle* because they are me, and I am them. They are so close to being born into awareness or from being taken from us by means of obliteration. *Now* is all there is and you are everything you need to be now.

Once you begin getting intimately familiar with yourself and studying your reactions as much as your responses, you will have a choice to make; you can decide you are broken or you can accept yourself as whole. If you believe you are broken you will believe you are powerless and will continue to find the words to justify your actions. If you decide you are whole you will admit that you have a choice in your actions and act as such.

I enjoy the mystic community in every religion. They tend to make room for other human beings. They are a little less enthralled with doctrine and are more interested in the connection to the One Source, wherever it is found. Through my research into these various mystical communities I came across the *Indigo Child* conversation. The thought that there are those amongst us born onto this planet to help this world step into consciousness and raise its frequency.

It is an interesting movement and I always enjoy the mystic perspective. A mystic will look at an autistic person, like myself, and not think "oh, poor man! Life must really be awful!" A mystic looks at everything with wonder and awe. They don't disregard science but understand it is interwoven with a plane we can't see with our eyes but can feel. There are many psychologists and doctors that are mystics. They use the unseen to enhance their physical practice, not replace it. This is where the east meets west in psychology, business, and medicine.

I make room, as a mystic, for the Psychologist to tell me I have *Autism Spectrum Disorder* and find wisdom in this definition and also find wisdom in the Indigo movement. Many, if not most, psychologists would be appalled by the term *Indigo Child*. Mainly because their predecessors would be. It might also put them out of a job or challenge them to work in new ways. It may challenge them to trust their own intuition. I believe Indigos are just people that have awaken to knowing they are not removed from the *Source of Infinite Intelligence*.

I would rather get my information from someone interested in and willing to consider all angles over someone who believes they are the answer or know them all. They are far too involved and enthralled in their ego to be of much help to me in where I am going. I still love the acorn and can learn from it but I have learned to revere a good oak tree when I so happen to find one. It is important to take these moments to rest in their shade.

Ralph Smart of *Infinite Waters* is an oak tree. He is one of these people that consider and make room for other people. His YouTube channel is fantastic for gooey people like me. Here he expands on these differences in a way that resonated with me. He says:

> *"Now, I studied psychology. I went to university at 17 years old. I also studied criminology. I've worked with*

people who have Autism and ADHD... Sometimes, we label people. I'm here to tell you; don't believe all of those labels. Those are gifted children... You care.

"This goes into autism. They care for animals, just like they care for humans. I used to work with an autistic child. He used to love animals! Absolutely love animals. Not just like a regular person 'oh, I love my dog!' No, no. Any animal he would see he would love it. He would treat it with compassion. That's just like the indigos.

"There's a reason why many indigos are vegan... Indigos honor all life. They don't think they are better than anyone else. When we talk about the ego, it even goes into what we are consuming." -Ralph Smart, Infinite Waters (Signs You are an Indigo)

    I won't dive any deeper into Indigo Children. There are *prickly people* and *gooey people*. There is a good chance I have lost a lot of my prickly people in the final chapter of this book. I am okay with this. They have reasons why everything is awful. Alan Watts said "Life itself can be thought of as a disease. It lingers on for years and ends with death."

We need both types of people for the other to know who they are. For too long we have lost our gooey people in business or they have just been severely under-represented. We don't have a guidebook for the alternative to prickly. There is a different way to practice business. I am not saying "do away with the prickly types". We need the prickly types! We need the money-hungry egoic people posing in front of their cars to recognize and see the inverse.

I don't know which type you are and I am fine with either. Neither are wrong. Just stop depending on others for your salvation. Stop depending on others to tell you who you are. You cannot teach someone to become a genius. You cannot teach someone to have a golden heart. You cannot give someone an ability to speak and rouse a crowd. They have to want to bring it out of themselves and until then they will only feign authenticity. They will speak words taught to them by others but will have no real feelings of their own.

Handing a person a degree, a certificate, or a diploma says "I am the expert and you have earned this right to be considered valid up unto this point." The problem with all of these certificates, degrees, and diplomas is that they continue to leave the person receiving them feeling that they somehow must continue to pursue this studying, as they have defined themselves as the student. They are living in the light of the ordained professor's approval of their existence.

They are all leading their various ferry boats across the rivers of enlightenment but it is only validation that is being quested for, knowledge and truth take a backseat. There is no *one way* to cross a river. There is no right way. Regard yourself as unofficial. Consider yourself an *expert in nothing* and a *student of everything*. Be curious about life, perpetually interested, willing to be influenced, and always open to being wrong. The second that one considers themselves an expert they have started their death. Experts are rough people to deal with. After all, they have a vested interest in being right.

Salvation lies within. It, again, is not something that must be quested for and is really only arrived at in the movies. People who seek the validation of others or for another person to grant them salvation will often seek it in degrees, sex, attention, becoming an expert, a killer, a winner, etc. and so forth. If we seek for someone else to tell us we are "enough" and they do not, we then look to take something from someone who can validate us. If we beat someone in a competition, or win a game, we feel we are better than someone else and are temporarily validated.

If you seek validation in others, or another person seeks to be validated by you, it can become exhausting. Many people believe that by focusing on the problems of another person that their problems will go away on their own. The receiver can often feel when a person is giving at a stretch and this causes guilt. If they don't realize the sacrifice, don't seem to grateful, or don't perform up to the unwritten standards to be worthy of the sacrifice it can cause resentment. After all, so much was sacrificed.

When people have *sacrificed* for their employees, team, kids, or the world they feel their approval is something that must be earned. They, as the people who have sacrificed, must approve of what their children, employees, spouse, or country has done with everything that has been sacrificed for them. What have they done that is worthy? Well, what are your numbers children? Let me review your performance. How many calls did you make? How many escrows did you close? What are your grades? I'm not sure that's good enough to get a cookie from me, the one who has sacrificed so much.

We often withhold approval when we feel like approval is something that must be earned by our parents, a parent, a boss, God, or that cold judgmental bastard living between our ears. We should not sacrifice in the hopes that greatness will come from the backs of everyone we have sacrificed everything for! If we give, let it be without strings attached. More importantly, let us not put off living our lives because we are too afraid of the judgement that will come from the inactive masses when we act!

When the soldier returns home from war and sees the complacency of the masses, the soldier is frustrated. *What have I sacrificed for?* The parent spends years raising a child who then becomes a drug-addict or simply less-than-stellar and they think "I sacrificed everything for this child". *How could they disappoint me?* The boss who sacrificed so much to get where they are, pays for their teams conveniences, and is angered by the fact that *they don't know what they're getting.* The problem is not that they have squandered the opportunity which was so generously set up for them. The problem is, somewhere along the way, the giver stopped giving and started sacrificing.

When we remember we enjoy giving it is easier to give without the expectation. When we realize we enjoy serving others because we are, in part, serving ourselves, all of the self-righteous, egoic reasons for serving dissipate and you are left with the joy of service. Why are we really doing these things? It connects us to humanity, giving to people, to our children, our country, to this world. Sacrificing alienates us from humanity. We become one step removed.

When you can give yourself validation you can more readily give it to others until they are ready to give it to themselves. We have been trained to believe that approval must be earned. I approve of you immediately without judgement. It is the burden of humanity to lose my trust. I love every person I meet because I love myself. Whose approval must I win? Who must validate me? Who must tell me I am worthy? I am.

I believe we did Jesus a great disservice by removing him from humanity. In the *Gospel According to John* an angry group of religious leaders had gathered around Jesus to stone him for being a heretic. Jesus works to explain his experience to these religious leaders in a way that they would understand, was supported by gospel, and would save his life without compromising his principles or message.

John 10:30

(30) "I and the Father are one." (31) At this, the Jews again picked up stones to stone Him. (32) But Jesus responded, "I have shown you many good works from the Father. For which of these do you stone Me?"
(33) "We are not stoning You for any good work," said the Jews, "but for blasphemy, because You, who are a man, declare Yourself to be God." (34) Jesus replied, "Is it not written in your Law: 'I have said you are gods'? (35) If he called them gods to whom the word of God came— and the Scripture cannot be broken— (36) then what about the One whom the Father sanctified and sent into the world? How then can you accuse Me of blasphemy for stating that I am the Son of God?" (37) If I am not doing the works of My Father, then do not believe Me. (38) But if I am doing them, even though you do not believe Me, believe the works themselves, so that you may know and understand

> *that the Father is in Me, and I am in the Father."*

Jesus understood scripture very well but there was not language to describe the experience he had at the time. It is still something we struggle to articulate. Alan Watts said "Jesus had a cosmic experience. Nirvana. Bodhi. Satori."(*Alan Watts When Man Becomes God.)*

> *"Bodhi, (Sanskrit and Pāli: 'awakening,' 'enlightenment'), in Buddhism, the final Enlightenment, which puts an end to the cycle of transmigration and leads to Nirvana, or spiritual release; the experience is comparable to the Satori of Zen Buddhism in Japan. The accomplishment of this 'awakening' transformed Siddhartha Gautama into a Buddha (an Awakened One).*
>
> *The final Enlightenment remains the ultimate ideal of all Buddhists, to be attained by ridding oneself of false beliefs and the hindrance of passions. This is achieved by following the course of spiritual discipline known as the Eightfold Path. Mahayana Buddhism, while embracing this ideal, places a high valuation on the*

> *compassion of the bodhisattva (one whose essence is bodhi), who postpones his own entrance into Nirvana in order to work for the salvation of all sentient beings." - Britannica.com*

When one realizes they are connected to everything and everyone they do not suddenly become detached from the world entirely, but they season life as they see fit. Attachments are the salt to stew! There is sustenance in every bite but the salt keeps us wanting more. We are all guilty, from time to time, of over seasoning our stew.

We don't know how to trigger enlightenment or travel to Nirvana. There are suggestions, but like the river crossing, there is no one way across the river. Alan Watts describes a friend of his who experienced Nirvana before his death by having a near death experience. He recalls the conversation he had with his friend while he was still alive.

> *"'I fear to speak to my friends of this but it was the most beautiful experience. I shall never be afraid of death. In fact, I recommend everyone to have a stroke.'"*

Nirvana, phew. The sigh of relief. You have made it. Phew. You do not have to go on. At this point you can ascend the body and float off into the clouds or spend the rest of your life meditating or you can postpone

Nirvana for the *salvation of all sentient beings*. You must first accept you will never get there and then you may choose to take your first step.

    I believe many people find Nirvana and postpone it for Bodhi through in and around the contemplation of suicide. I have been suicidal or deeply depressed throughout much of my life. It was only through deep consideration of suicide that I realized how preposterous it was. We can start over in every moment but we keep ourselves, quite literally, chained to the past.

    On the show *After Life* by Ricky Gervais on Netflix Ricky plays a suicidal and depressed local newspaper writer who has recently lost his wife to cancer. I enjoy his intellectual and cutting humor. At one point he says something like *"I'm kind of like a super hero. I figure I could always kill myself if it doesn't work out."* Brilliant. True. Hilarious. Humor often has its finger on the femoral artery of tragedy and enlightenment.

    If you do the things you want and need to do, without the unnecessary attachments, suicide becomes a humorous meditation for being unattached to life's long-term plans but living life for now because, after all, we can always kill ourselves if it doesn't work out! It makes it more fun, and humorous, when you can describe your life in this sort of unattached way. *Well, I can go do the dishes or I can blow my brains out!*

    Much of what was important becomes ridiculous and what was ridiculous suddenly becomes important.

The competition, the desire to be #1, the hustle, all irrelevant. Even bothersome. The desire to experience now; pressing, wonderful, liberating. For now is all we have, my ascended friends. Breathe it in deeply.

We don't kill ourselves because we want to live! How simple. When we decide we want to live then we go on living. While we are here we might as well do some good for some people because it feels good giving! It feels good to serve because it is self-serving in all the best ways!

What is it I need to be for whom? What must I accomplish and why? Being anything other than me in any moment prevents me from connecting to another human being and authentically getting to know myself. It creates the egoic divide. You are you, and I am me, and we are different. Agents comparing numbers, showing one another their paychecks. *I am this, I am from there, and I am not that, I would never this.*

If we must judge ourselves let it be by a better litmus test. What are we doing for others? How can we be of service? You must only be *you* to be complete. Remove all of what you are not. Season to taste. You must only say "I am". Everything else is a hinderance. Everything else is packaging. With that acceptance comes Nirvana, the phew, the sigh of relief. I am enough. I made it. Anything that comes after "I am" removes you from God, everything that is infinite, and all that which is yes.

Psalm 82

> *"(1) God presides in the great assembly; he renders judgment among the 'gods':*
>
> *(2) "'How long will you defend the unjust and show partiality to the wicked?*
>
> *(3) Defend the weak and the fatherless; uphold the cause of the poor and the oppressed.*
>
> *(4) Rescue the weak and the needy; deliver them from the hand of the wicked.*
>
> *(5) The 'gods' know nothing, they understand nothing. They walk about in darkness; all the foundations of the earth are shaken.'"*
>
> *(6) "I said, 'You are "gods"; you are all sons of the Most High.'*
>
> *(7) But you will die like mere mortals; you will fall like every other ruler."*
>
> *(8) Rise up, O God, judge the earth, for all the nations are your inheritance."*

With responsibility comes a need for a response. Yes, there is wickedness in the world. Much of it is caused by the wickedness of Gods who are acting like children. They don't know the power they possess and choose to use it exalting themselves or making others small. In *Psalms 82*, just as in *John 10* we see it again, *"You are Gods"*. So, *"Rise up, O God, judge the earth for the nations are your inheritance."*

This idea is supported and affirmed not only in the Christian and Jewish texts, but also in the Quran. The idea that God is everywhere in every person we meet, and in us.

Surah Al-Baqarah 2:115

"2) To Allah belongs the East and the West; wherever you turn, this is Allah's face. Allah is All-Encompassing (Omnipresent) and All-Knowing."

Surah Qaf 50:16

"And indeed We have created man, and We know whatever thoughts his inner self develops, and We are closer to him than (his) jugular vein."

Dick Gregory, during an interview (which I cannot find, so this is an indirect quote here), told the interviewer something along the lines of this; "If I took your sister out for a date and I wanted to show her I cared about her I would buy her something from Target and then I might go down to Bloomingdales, because I know someone down there, and have them wrap it up really nicely for me in fancy wrapping paper."

We are obsessed with the "wrapping paper" as a society and care much less about what is inside. We will swallow just about anything if it is packaged nicely for us. Look no further than the food we eat. Wrapping paper is race, gender, things, stuff, cars, hair, tattoos, houses, it is anything that wraps us up and makes us feel separate from humanity. If we define ourselves by our race, our homes, our service, our background, we remove ourselves from the oneness. The fact that I have served makes me no different than any other person. The fact that I lived in poverty makes me no different than any other person. More than anything what will paint who I am for the world to see is the perspective I carry with me throughout my life.

We are not the sum of our experiences. If this were the case we would not have such a wide variance of personalities within one household. If this were the case, brothers would be more or less the same. Twins would be, more or less, the same but this is not the case. Some people believe they have a choice and they can change their stars while others believe they are an insignificant piece of meat to be acted upon in a meaningless world. Both are right.

Rarely do you find lasting ascension in places of peace and tranquility. Most of the POWs who returned home from Vietnam became better men than the ones that left for combat. It is not unique to this community to have been better people post-trauma than the people they were before the trauma. We have only one of two ways to experience trauma; we can grow from it or we can allow it to inhibit us, therefore causing a disorder. Post-Traumatic Stress Disorder or Post-Traumatic Growth? The choice is yours and it is simple and it is a choice.

We do not realize we are God, or have God within us, or are one with God while lighting candles and incense and chanting on top of a mountain. The ego loves to play the enlightenment game. If we are celebrating our enlightenment or bragging about how often or for how long we meditate our ego has taken over our spiritual journey. We all see the egoic spiritual or religious leaders being celebrated for being spiritual or religious. Okay, now what? What will you do with God's Hands now that you have realized they are your own?

People often realize God is within when we, or someone else, are in pain and we ascend the body. Pain is one of the largest gifts I receive when I can properly utilize it when it comes. I spent years of my life in pain. I got to a point where I expected to be in pain and I was. I started preparing my body for pain when I walked and kept muscles tense and ready for the jolt that would come, without reason, as I am walking. I have spots in my foot that are numb and a nodule that will suddenly make it feel as if I am stepping on a Lego when it slides under my heel.

It used to be, when this pain would come, I would suddenly become angry or feel very sorry for myself. There were other times I would push down on my heel, ferociously, wanting this thing to cause me as much pain as possible hoping if I did it right, it would go away eventually. I've even considered making cuts into various parts of my foot to relieve the pain. There are times it feels overwhelming and exhausting.

    When the pain comes now I simply try not to mention it. The pain reminds me to be present. It reminds me my time here on earth is limited. I want to live my life, not spend my life sitting on the sidelines making excuses for why I have not lived. This may be my last go-round here on planet earth. I do believe I have been here before. This time I want to see it, experience it, and emerge myself in life. I have little desire to travel or to see beautiful places. I crave to place my hands on humanity one last time, in every moment. To witness the dance, to breathe in the air, to live without being paralyzed by the thought of living one last time and maybe jot a few things down before I go.

    Go where you think God is needed. I hear people say "God is needed in the schools" then volunteer. I hear other people talk about "the pains in the world" and then mock God for not being all powerful. The *limiting beliefs* are on them. They will continue to think this world is for God to fix and they will continue to miss the point entirely. Do what you think God must do. Or did you think you were put here to be entertained?

    There are people that experience Nirvana while incarcerated, being trafficked, during a near-death experience, or while doing seemingly inane tasks after questing for enlightenment for years. Suddenly it clicks. They are at One. They no longer wish to take, to destroy, or to compete. They may play games competitively but, for the most part, they live with joy! You may still have fun with business. You may still enjoy the competition but enjoy it as a game. It is not war.

The ego will say "it is not a game! This is how I feed my family!" The ego is terrified. It thinks it's needed. It believes it must be heard and recognized. There are wars in which you may get involved, if you so choose to do so, but you will find enough trouble simply trying to do the right thing in this country, in this world, in your own life. This is not a new occurrence.

The people of the world today are not so different from the people of the past. We have not learned all of these lessons that were supposed to accompany civility. Just because a society is civilized does not mean it is enlightened. Civil societies are often egoic societies. We were never meant to be civilized. What religious or political leader won you over with how civil they were? A lot of pain has been caused in the name of *civility*.

One of my favorite things about many spiritual leaders is that they are not civil when the time has passed for civility. This is why I enjoy the *True Warrior* when I meet one in the wild and the principles laid out for the Samurai in the *Bushido*. Jesus could be civil when the time came for it but he also possessed the ability to be quite hostile.

Whenever anyone does too much good they will be questioned. They will be put to the fire and we will seek to destroy them. Whether through media and the press or social media and the peers. Either by reputation or in form.

Nothing will stir a drifting soul resting on the laurels of their ego like a person doing good without reason. Disagree with me? Just look to history to see the way we destroy those who do good. They test us and comfortable people do not like to be tested.

The moments in which Jesus quotes scripture to rebuke or debate the religious elite are treasures. In the *Gospel According to Mark* Jesus is, once again, doing good works when trouble seeks him out in the form of religious leaders. Once again, they do not come in peace.

Mark 11 & 12

(27) After their return to Jerusalem, Jesus was walking in the temple courts, and the chief priests, scribes, and elders came up to Him. (28) "By what authority are You doing these things?" they asked. "And who gave You the authority to do them?" (29) "I will ask you one question," Jesus replied, "and if you answer Me, I will tell you by what authority I am doing these things. (30) The baptism of John, was it from heaven or from men? Answer Me!" (31) They deliberated among themselves what they should answer: "If we say, 'From heaven,' He

will ask, 'Why then did you not believe him?' (32) But if we say, 'From men'..." they were afraid of the people, for they all held that John truly was a prophet. (33) So they answered Him, *"We do not know." And Jesus replied, "Neither will I tell you by what authority I am doing these things."*

The Parable of the Wicked Tenants

(1) Then Jesus began to speak to them in parables: "A man planted a vineyard. He put a wall around it, dug a wine vat, and built a watchtower. Then he rented it out to some tenants and went away on a journey. (2) At harvest time, he sent a servant to the tenants to collect his share of the fruit of the vineyard. (3) But they seized the servant, beat him, and sent him away empty-handed. (4) Then he sent them another servant, and they struck him over the head and treated him shamefully. (5) He sent still another, and this one they killed. He sent many others; some they beat and others they killed. (6) Finally, having one beloved son, he sent him to them. 'They will respect my son,' he said (7) But the tenants said to one another,

'This is the heir; come, let us kill him, and the inheritance will be ours.' (8) So they seized the son, killed him, and threw him out of the vineyard. (9) What then will the owner of the vineyard do? He will come and kill those tenants, and will give the vineyard to others. (10) Have you never read this Scripture: 'The stone the builders rejected has become the cornerstone. (11) This is from the Lord, and it is marvelous in our eyes'?" (12) At this, the leaders sought to arrest Jesus, for they knew that He had spoken this parable against them. But fearing the crowd, they left Him and went away."

The crowd won the day. As is often the case, as it was on the day Jesus was crucified. We will not win all of our fights but we must not be willing to back down from them. How many servants, sons, and daughters must be killed who are doing good work? *As many as it takes.* If even half of us committed to peace with a tenth of the veracity of Dr. Martin Luther King Jr. our problems would be solved within a few weeks.

Safety is not a guarantee in any holy book that I know of, in fact it is quite the opposite. A person who believes in serving humanity does not ascend fear or pain in the body, that would be taking something away from them. They understand the temporary state and what is truly important to The Oneness. There are hearts that will continue to beat past my exit of this world. There is much at stake if you choose to partake in the liberation of human beings in the flesh. It may be required that you get un-civilized.

One of my favorite Christian books is *The Barbarian Way* by Erwin Raphael McManus. He's a Los Angeles Pastor in the Mosaic Church, a speaker, and an author. He writes about John The Baptist, this recognized prophet that was revered by the people, the name Jesus cited when he was under fire from the established religious leaders of the time.

> *"He was clearly not a fan of the established religious leaders. His nickname for the Pharisees and Sadducees, who were the pinnacle of the religious elite, was 'brood of vipers'. Nope that was not a term of endearment. And I think it's important to note that his fire-and-brimstone message was entirely directed towards the religious, not the irreligious. He was a barbarian in the midst of civilization. And frankly the civilization made him sick. He had no patience for domesticated religionists who were drowning in their own self-righteousness."*

> *"Oh, and by the way, he had no formal education, no degrees. His occupation was prophet, and his mailing address was the wilderness."*

    Alan Watts said "To be an authority today in the academic world, you have to have the proper paperwork." If I were to open a facility to help veterans out of my home the government would come and say "by what authority do you do these things?" They would ask for the proper paperwork and see if I had paid the proper fees. Our freedom comes with so many constraints that we are questioned and must pay fees, get permits, and establish foundations in order to do good things.
    The time is not so different now from when religious leaders and the political elite were so intertwined they were encouraging people to stone their opposition in the streets. In fact, the time is rather similar. We just think we are more civilized and so we destroy people through media.
    These religious leaders came with the power of the state to seize Jesus. They wanted to know; Who said that before? Who wrote that? It can't be true if it wasn't written somewhere previously or proven. We want evidence. We want proof. Spend your life proving things... Have fun with that! There will always be someone looking to prove the inverse. Always another expert to debate. Speak by your own authority. Declare your truth. It takes courage to speak and stand on your own words.

Alan Watts says this is why there are so many "books about books about books about books." No one says anything new. He also said "To speak with originality is to speak with authority" Now, I'm quoting a guy about speaking with originality! I have trouble standing on my own word as well.

This final concept, that you are God, that I am God, or at least that God lives within us, is the final stage in enlightenment for you to wake up, stand up, realize who you are, and speak with and engage the world as an Authority of The Oneness.

You cannot be an authority at home by yourself in your closet. You may do your studying, resting, and feeling connected to the Oneness but I urge you to engage. To not engage is cowardice. There is no love there. You will only find fear in your inability to move. You do not need the whole plan, you must only know the next step in order to take one.

I hesitate to say "must" but in order to achieve joy or satisfaction with your time spent on Earth I strongly encourage you to engage the world with the talents you are cultivating, or have cultivated, whatever those talents may be! For "where two or three gather in My name, there am I with them." I am not telling you to go into the trenches, where you are uncomfortable, but live the life that is burning in your heart. Whatever that life is and whatever that life looks like, just don't spend it alone. You don't need anyone to validate your movement. You don't even need to move with others.

Solitude is wonderful. I enjoy my solitude but we did not come here to walk alone for a hundred years.

Matthew 18

(18) Truly I tell you, whatever you bind on earth will be bound in heaven, and whatever you loose on earth will be loosed in heaven. (19) Again, I tell you truly that if two of you on the earth agree about anything you ask for, it will be done for you by My Father in heaven. (20) For where two or three gather together in My name, there am I with them."

  The Kingdom of Heaven is at hand and yet we wait to get there. Don't wait to get there. Roll up your sleeves and get to work. It is here. Stop waiting for this grand reunification with God and see him/her in your clients, your children, and in every person you meet.
  The fragile enlightened one, tucked away, meditating on top of a mountain or in their tranquility room reading holy books, fasting, and surrounding themselves with other holy people does little to raise consciousness or the frequency of the world. Is this real enlightenment? Can a head exist without being connected to the body?
  We must be around others to find real peace and what better way than in the service of the human body? Whether you are helping people find homes, are

a doctor, or are volunteering, do all of these things as a spiritual practice. In service of the One Mind and One Body.

There are many functions of the human body. Many of which take place without us being aware or fully conscious of them. Some take out the literal trash, others the figurative trash. Some fight infection, others relieve pain. Some write new programming, and others consume it. It takes all parts working together, somewhat effectively, for the body to maintain health. When the body attacks itself, which happens from time to time, it causes disease. Participate with the human body but do so consciously. Do so with your eyes open. One cannot be the hammer and not also be the nail.

When we look at the soldiers that carried out the orders to crucify Jesus or the soldiers that rounded up Jewish people or the police being sent to arrest a person unlawfully, none of them considered they had a choice to say "no" but this is where real courage comes into play.

I remember serving in the Marine Corps during the *Occupy Wall Street* protests in 2011. The protests were a frequent area of conversation amongst the Marines, who were trained in riot control, and many were chomping at the bit, hoping for an opportunity to get orders to New York. During this time, in the back of a large troop carrying vehicle, the conversation came up again but it took a more serious turn as someone asked "would you shoot the protestors if you were given the order?" The answer was an overwhelming "yes" with only a few dissenting voices.

When you see another human being as separate from you, you are more willing to destroy them. I explained the ramifications of killing Americans for protesting in the streets and talked about the Boston Massacre, about the National Guard opening fire on college students, and was met with rebuttal after rebuttal justifying the actions of the government.

Eckhart Tolle was interviewed on the *Rubin Report* and explained why, when Jesus was crucified, he said "Father, forgive them, for they do not know what they are doing." (Matthew 23:34). Jesus knew that the men who crucified him, mocked him, and offered him sour wine while he was on the cross were asleep. They weren't fully conscious people. They were not awake.

I love oak trees but I will spend much of my life with acorns. By the time a person reaches adulthood they have learned so much that isn't true. The goal is to enlighten parents, so they can enlighten others. If we can effectively enlighten parents, and they can fight their own demons, they pass less of them along and we can raise children who are spiritually awake.

Business is a medium I enjoy working in because it is a parable for everything else. If I can help a person realize, affirm, or give a person words for understanding they are whole and complete and one with God, then their entire life will be better.

In Hebrew "son" means "nature of" so "Son of God" would be "Nature of God". If we are all "Children of God", which is the point Jesus made several times throughout the bible, then what is preventing us from acting the part? Well for one we believe Jesus was capable of so much that we are not. We are, after all, *just men.*

In the profound and brilliant article entitled *Everyone is God* by author Wai H. Tsang he writes;

> *"Many people are familiar with the idea of the 'Christ within'. In Hinduism's premier holy text the Bhagavad Gita we have the 'Krishna within', and the Koran tells us that Allah is 'closer than your jugular vein'. The Buddhist scriptures talk about the Buddha within and correspondingly the Adi Granth, which is the Sikh holy text, describes that 'the one God is all pervading and alone dwells in the Mind'. Though many religious people know the idea that God is to be found within them, they imagine that somehow a small and divided piece of God is inside them or perhaps that all it means is that there is some aspect of God within us. However other passages in the scriptures of the World's religions also clearly state that God is indeed within us, but also that God is undivided, indivisible and always one.*

The following are several scriptures from various world religions to support this thesis. Some of these were brought to my attention through Wai H. Tsang's article, others came up during my research for this book;

Bhagavad Gita 6:29

"The man whose self is disciplined in yoga, whose perception is the same everywhere, sees himself in all creatures and all creatures in himself. For the man who sees me in everything and everything in me, I am not lost for him and he is not lost for me."

Luke 17:21

"The kingdom of God does not come with your careful observation, nor will people say, 'Here it is' or 'There it is,' because the kingdom of God is within you."

Quran 50:16

'Man is my mystery and I am his mystery, for I am he himself and he is also I myself' - Muhammad, Hadith Qudsi

Now, the entirety of *Matthew Chapter 6* summed up so much of what is written about in this book that I could not find one piece or another to choose from. As Christianity is the Religion of the West, I have decided to include the entire Chapter because it is, quite perfect in its entirety.

Matthew Chapter 6

(1) "Be especially careful when you are trying to be good so that you don't make a performance out of it. It might be good theater, but the God who made you won't be applauding. (2) When you do something for someone else, don't call attention to yourself. You've seen them in action, I'm sure - 'playactors' I call them - treating prayer meeting and street corner alike as a stage, acting compassionate as long as someone is watching, playing to the crowds. They get applause, true, but that's all they get. (3) When you help someone out, don't think about how it looks. (4) Just do it - quietly and unobtrusively. That is the way your God, who conceived you in love, working behind the scenes, helps you out. (5) And when you come before God, don't turn that into a theatrical production either. All these people

making a regular show out of their prayers, hoping for stardom! Do you think God sits in a box seat? (6) Here's what I want you to do: Find a quiet, secluded place so you won't be tempted to role-play before God. Just be there as simply and honestly as you can manage. The focus will shift from you to God, and you will begin to sense his grace. (7) The world is full of so-called prayer warriors who are prayer-ignorant. They're full of formulas and programs and advice, peddling techniques for getting what you want from God. (8) Don't fall for that nonsense. This is your Father you are dealing with, and he knows better than you what you need. (9) With a God like this loving you, you can pray very simply. Like this: Our Father in heaven, Reveal who you are. (10) Set the world right; Do what's best - as above, so below. (11) Keep us alive with three square meals. (12) Keep us forgiven with you and forgiving others. (13) Keep us safe from ourselves and the Devil. You're in charge! You can do anything you want! You're ablaze in beauty! Yes. Yes. Yes. (14) In prayer there is a connection between what

God does and what you do. You can't get forgiveness from God, for instance, without also forgiving others. (15) If you refuse to do your part, you cut yourself off from God's part. (16) When you practice some appetite-denying discipline to better concentrate on God, don't make a production out of it. It might turn you into a small-time celebrity but it won't make you a saint. (17) If you 'go into training' inwardly, act normal outwardly. Shampoo and comb your hair, brush your teeth, wash your face. (18) God doesn't require attention-getting devices. He won't overlook what you are doing; he'll reward you well. A Life of God-Worship (19) Don't hoard treasure down here where it gets eaten by moths and corroded by rust or - worse! - stolen by burglars. (20) Stockpile treasure in heaven, where it's safe from moth and rust and burglars. (21) It's obvious, isn't it? The place where your treasure is, is the place you will most want to be, and end up being. (22) Your eyes are windows into your body. If you open your eyes wide in wonder and belief, your body fills up with light. (23) If you live squinty-eyed in greed and distrust, your body is a dank cellar. If you pull the blinds on your windows, what a dark life you will have! (24) You can't worship two gods at once. Loving one god, you'll end up hating the other. Adoration of one feeds contempt for the other. You can't worship God and Money both. (25) If you decide for God, living a life of God-worship, it follows that you don't fuss about what's on the table at mealtimes or whether the clothes in your closet are in fashion. There is far more to your life than the food you put in your stomach, more to your outer appearance than the clothes you hang on your body. (26) Look at the birds, free and unfettered, not tied down to a job description, careless in the care of God. And you count far more to him than birds. (27) Has anyone by fussing in front of the mirror ever gotten taller by so much as an inch? (28) All this time and money wasted on fashion - do you think it makes that much difference? Instead of looking at the fashions, walk out into the fields and look at the wildflowers. They never primp or shop, (29) but have you ever

> *seen color and design quite like it? The ten best-dressed men and women in the country look shabby alongside them. (30) If God gives such attention to the appearance of wildflowers - most of which are never even seen - don't you think he'll attend to you, take pride in you, do his best for you? (31) What I'm trying to do here is to get you to relax, to not be so preoccupied with getting, so you can respond to God's giving."*

Ascending the ego actually brings you closer to God. Not by being little, or insignificant, but by opening your eyes to let the light in. Seeing things as they actually are so that you may place your hands on them. Don't get so caught up in job descriptions that you forget to serve or think it is someone else's job.

Anyone who can say "I am" without identifying further will find themselves practicing Bodhicitta because they will have ascended the ego. In addition, it will feel like Mushin. No mind. Peace. Fingers on strings. Hands healing bodies. It will feel good and right. We go, once again, to Alan Watts;

> *"To know that you are god is to know that you are completely with this universe. If you don't know that, you feel alien, you feel a stranger, you feel hostile. And so you beat everything up*

and seek to bend it to your will." (Alan Watts — You Are God)

We all see people out there seeking to bend the world, their industry, their families to their will. They want subordinates and competitors and they are threatened by everything. I know this state well because I lived there for a while and slip into it from time to time. It is egoic. It is *how can I win* vs. *how can I be of service?* I started out with the mindset of service but ego took over through fear. I had to forget myself.

Quran 59:19

"And be not like those who forgot Allah, so He made them forget themselves. Those are the defiantly disobedient."

When we forget ourselves, we forget God. I have always had a servant's heart but fear and pain flooded in and I crumbled. I experienced business death and eventually the first crumblings of the ego I had created to keep myself separate and safe from the world. Safely tucked away, untouchable.

I did not realize God is within me, or that I am God, in the heights of success. I realized it in the pitfalls of failure. I also realized, through this awakening, that we get opportunities to help others see. If God is within everyone, waiting to be awakened, are we also not creators of Gods? Do we create heaven and hell like Gods? I would certainly say we do. Heaven is now. Hell is the damage we cause when we are, or were, unconscious and what we pay for with the pain we caused when we realize we caused it, or what others continue to pay for our unconsciousness.

If we yell at our children because we are irritated about something that has nothing to do with them, this is hell. When we punish ourselves for it afterward, this is hell. If we don't correct this behavior our children will continue to pay the price as they will live lives in hell around us. The anxiety that is developed will outlive our presence in their lives.

Often our thoughts about God are our thoughts of ourselves. If we feel out of control in our lives: *God is just some guy with an anthill.* If we are acting out of spite and hold it in our hearts: *God is a vengeful God*. If we feel like life is good and plentiful: *God provides.* We remove much of our influence over our life and God makes us forget ourselves.

If you say "God is without meaning and terrible." I would say "you are right". If you said "What a maleficent beast god is!" I would say "your thoughts on god have more to do with you, in your current state, than anything else." If you say "God is powerful and can move mountains" I would say "you certainly can. What mountain do you wish to move?"

Jesus, as Alan Watts says "was made irrelevant by being kicked upstairs". Jesus tells us, time and time again, both in his own words and by quoting scripture that God is within us, just as He was within Jesus. He tells his disciples this, once again, knowing that his time here on earth is limited.

John 14:8

(8) Philip said to Him, "Lord, show us the Father, and that will be enough for us." (9) Jesus replied, "Philip, I have been with you all this time, and still you do not know Me? Anyone who has seen Me has seen the Father. How can you say, 'Show us the Father'? (10) Do you not believe that I am in the Father and the Father is in Me? The words I say to you, I do not speak on My own. Instead, it is the Father dwelling in Me, performing His works. (11) Believe Me that I am in the Father and the Father is in Me—or at least believe on account of the works themselves. (12) Truly, truly, I tell you, whoever believes in Me will also do the works that I am doing. He will do even greater things than these, because I am going to the Father. (13) And I will do whatever you ask in My name, so that the Father may be glorified in the Son. (14) If you ask Me anything in My name, I will do it. (15) If you love Me, you will keep My commandments. (16) And I will ask the Father, and He will give you

> *another Advocate to be with you forever— (17) the Spirit of truth. The world cannot receive Him, because it neither sees Him nor knows Him. But you do know Him, for He abides with you and will be in you. (18) I will not leave you as orphans; I will come to you. (19) In a little while, the world will see Me no more, but you will see Me. Because I live, you also will live. (20) On that day you will know that I am in My Father, and you are in Me, and I am in you."*

Here Jesus is pleading with his disciples to understand that the Father, that resides within Jesus, is also in them! Yet the disciples, who have witnessed all of these works, ask for Jesus to show them God in form! Jesus had experienced this enlightenment and wished to share it with his disciples. He had seen the light.

Sometimes when people "see the light" or experience Nirvana, or Bodhi, they then are "called" or feel compelled to act based on their newfound awareness. They may get involved in something radical or simply live life more aware. You do not need to seek to be Jesus, or Martin Luther King Jr. or Mother Teresa, those people have already been here. Just be less of who you are not and you will find Who resides beneath the ego.

Mother Teresa said;

> *"Stay where you are. Find your own Calcutta. Find the sick, the suffering, and the lonely, right where you are — in your own homes and in your own families, in homes and in your workplaces and in your schools. You can find Calcutta all over the world, if you have eyes to see. Everywhere, wherever you go, you find people who are unwanted, unloved, uncared for, just rejected by society — completely forgotten, completely left alone." -Mother Teresa*

You do not need to travel to some "poor" country to find the hurting and disenchanted. Look no further than your own city, your own community, your own home. Follow the example of Jesus while still respecting him as a man of flesh who transcended this earth. By making him the one and only Son of God, and denying that we are "Children of God" or "Gods" we are removing our influence over the world we live in.

The Ultimate Plan still belongs to God but I can take inspired action to influence the outcome and act as God's Hand. I am not asking God to reveal his plans to me but taking one step at a time with as much awareness as I can muster. By respecting our place in the process as influential, not powerless, we can understand free-will. The human mind, in our form, can only work at three things at once. I prefer to have the Business Plan with the Infinite Intelligence and I will act today based on the task that is in front of me. This is *faith*.

Buddha is one who awakens from the illusion of some of the sorrow that is from the thought there is something to get from life. That throughout the course of time *it will be alright*. Everything is *alright* now.

A Buddhist Monk is sometimes called a *Sramana*. This is closely related to the word *Shaman*. A Shaman is *a holy man in a culture that is still hunting*. There is a strong and important difference between a *Shaman* and a *Priest*. Priests are ordained. They are recognized through proper paperwork, performing and understanding doctrine, and studying religious writings. They are the Company Men of God. While a Shaman spends time alone and connects directly with the *Spirit of truth*. They are not recognized, nor do many of them desire to be. They only wish to be at one with the world in whatever capacity is necessary.

It's very difficult to find out who you are when you are constantly surrounded with other people. This is why, when Jesus was most under attack from this world, he sought moments of solitude and silence. He didn't seek the counsel of his peers. I believe when Jesus went into the desert to fast he didn't come back until he experienced *Nirvana*. When he had, he came back speaking from the One Source. Nirvana has been described by Alan Watts as "Phew. I have at last discovered that I don't have to survive." When Jesus accepted this, he came back to his disciples after first having his ego tempted by the devil.

When he came back he didn't go around asking to be recognized for fasting for 40 days and nights and start bragging about how hard it was over a large steak and a full cup of wine. He got to preaching what he had learned in solitude. In this moment, I believe he experienced *Bodhi* and he chose to forgo Nirvana to pursue the awakening of other sentient beings.

Buddha became enlightened when he gave up trying to take the Kingdom of Heaven by storm. It can be considered a "goal" to reach this state of enlightenment but it is not a state that can be reached permanently but momentarily ascended to, and once there, it is a more regular occurrence of staying for prolonged periods of time. It is a state of mind. Siddhartha Gautama attained, Jesus attained, and we all can attain.

What is the goal? If the goal is to make the world a better place. Do just that with how you make people feel. You can give all the things in the world to a person and make them feel small and weak. You can give food and take, in exchange, their pride and dignity. This is why I worked so hard with every team I have ever had on scripting. It's not what you say, or how you say it, but how the person feels when hearing it.

> *"I've learned that people will forget what you said, people will forget what you did, but people will never forget how you made them feel." -Maya Angelou*

The feeling sustains, which is why we should start with the feeling at the heart of everything we do. This is not to become over-enthusiastic while screaming affirmations, nor is it to stay in a mode of self-effacing drive where nothing is ever good enough. Rather clear the slate.

Emotions are not negative or positive but they are what puts our energy into motion. We would not move to create or accomplish great things without emotion, without some attachments, without some salt in our stew. Emotion is the fossil fuel of the emotional world. You can't run on emotion alone but it is put there to put the body in motion. It is strongly encouraged to evolve, though not necessary. I will not say "you must", but in order to attain enlightenment one cannot run on emotion alone, nor can they deny its existence.

We can get lost in emotion when we don't use it properly or do not seek to understand it. The largest philosophical question for many becomes whether or not to kill yourself. If you don't, what are you going to do with all of this life you have left over?

The Government, because they have declared themselves God, is getting more involved in the suicide conversation. They have leaned on psychology as God and are now picking *winners*. What life is worth the candle? If someone is looking for permission to kill themselves it is not the states responsibility to determine who can and cannot follow through with this act. Whose flame is worth the candle and who would be better left for parts.

Why the government, why psychologists, or coaches, or team leads? Do we not know ourselves best? If we know ourselves best, mastery over self comes. Enjoy your guides, seek mentorship in different schools of thought, but let nothing stand between you and The Truth. The answer to the world's problems lie within us. They must not be begged for, sacrificed for, bargained for, paid for, or anything other form of nonsense. We must only act on our truth. In order to understand our truth, we must remove all of what we are not.

> *"The Prophet, upon him blessings and peace, was asked: 'Who among people knows his Lord best?' He replied: 'Whoever knows himself best.'" -Living Islam. "Whoever knows himself, he knows his Lord" - GFH*

Alan Watts said "Men have free will to the extent that he knows who he is." Mastery comes from knowing yourself. The winner in a fight is often not the person who plans best for his opponent but the one who has best prepared himself. One of my favorite quotes that can be applied to life, Zen, and business is by Mike Tyson; "Everybody has a plan until they get punched in the mouth."

If you have true mastery of yourself, as the True Warrior is conscious of the Bushido, you may find that you spend significantly less time in combat. After all, much of the art of the *Art of War* is how to avoid war.

You will feel less threatened by others successes and you will probably spend more time healing and helping others than destroying the competition. When you can set the ego aside, your time is no longer worth a dollar amount, it is much more valuable than something so trivial.

With knowing who you are comes recognizing your abilities and using them to serve. Not only your *special abilities* in which your ego declares yourself the best and most valuable but you will feel compelled to serve with your hands because you have hands, your mind because you have a mind, and your heart because it beats within you. When we serve, let it be with all of us.

Enlightenment doesn't necessarily mean one ascends the body and becomes completely devoid of all attachments. You still have attachments. They are what keep you here. One of my favorite stories about Zen and enlightenment takes places where there is a master who is living out in some place of enlightenment and a western class of students travels to see him and stay with the master for a few days. The first day they find he smokes and they are perturbed, the second that he gets angry and they are disappointed, and the third that he has a girlfriend and they leave this place of enlightenment completely outraged and disenchanted.

These are our attachments. The pleasures of the flesh are not wicked or awful. They are the salt to our stew. They are only awful to the extent in which you make them your king and serve them. Then your stew becomes overly seasoned and ill to taste.

One of my favorite things about Jesus was his anger. It kept him here. It showed his very human exhaustion. His desire to reach people. His ascension was made all the more beautiful because he was able to ascend his attachments to his own body and offer forgiveness during his final moments. His anger made him salty. It made Jesus real and his story worth telling.

Our attachments keep us here. They keep us grounded in the earth and in time. Our children, spouse, job, home, cars, cities, coffee, cigarettes, service, volunteerism, love, hate, time, music, sunsets, friends, dreams, food, anything and everything in this realm is an attachment. Today, I am a salty stew that is grateful that his wife likes salty stew. She has an awful palate and I am the fortunate benefactor.

I am attached but I am careful to choose my attachments with my eyes open. By being selective with our attachments and discerning what is and is not worth our time spent here, we can more easily rise above the egoic principles that we were put here to be entertained and that the world must make us comfortable.

When we can rise above these principles we will be more readily able to fall in love with each moment and each person standing in front of us. We will see them as they truly are; as perfect as the stars they were made from.

I have a tendency to love people without rhyme or reason and, at times, it doesn't make me a great businessman. When I meet people the first time they will often recall how I treated them as if I knew them my whole life. I love everyone I meet when I am at my best. I call you *my brother*, or *my sister*, because I cannot call you *my heart*. To meet new people is to meet a new piece of my heart that will forever continue to beat in this world outside of me. I love people *now* because there is no other time or way to love them.

I got myself into trouble because I was giving from a place of a deficit. I was living in fear and it overwhelmed me. I didn't understand my vehicle. I tell people "if I carried my net worth in my pocket, I would give it away". I have come to realize I am autistic. I only carry a limited amount of cash in my pocket. If I am accused of anything it will be I gave too much, when I had too little, and my life spiraled out of whack. My ego thought I was needed so desperately. That I was the answer for so many people. I am not needed by anyone or anything. Life will go on without me. Therefore I am free to serve everyone.

If I died tomorrow that would be okay. I am not the salvation of the world but I hold the key to my own Kingdom of Heaven and it is here on Earth, every day in every moment that I am conscious enough to see it. I am planting seeds for trees under which I may never enjoy the shade. One day I will give myself to these trees and they will grow beyond me. Some of them are my children and I hope many of them are strangers. My death will be more birth, just like my business death was, as it helped to soil the valley and I am happy with what came from my death. Something better. The success of more people who were capable of success!

Jerry Linenger is an astronaut who has spent over 5 months in space, an author, and one of the eight speakers for *One Strange Rock*, a 10-part documentary series narrated by Will Smith and directed by Darren Aronofsky. *One Strange Rock* is about this incredible planet we live on. Linenger explains how crucial death is for life to continue on earth. He says;

> *"You know you really need death to have this complex world that we have. It, sort of, is the arbitrator. By having death you have new life taking its place and probably an improved form of that life."* -Jerry Linenger

I have experienced business death. For many of us in the western world this is as close to death as we get in our lifetimes while still walking away with a heartbeat. My death gave way for others to thrive, to make a name for themselves, and continue to improve the systems, lifestyles, and the industry I practice in. Our local business hemisphere is different than it was five years ago, in part, because of my life and death in it. I hope my reemergence will be effective in setting some of the ground work for substantive change in this industry and the others surrounding it.

I have touched on business death quite a few times in this book. Some will be driven mad by it, others will be controlled by it, some will quit, and others will emerge better, more fully realized versions of themselves.

Facing real death, in many ways, was more concrete. People went on living or they were killed. In business death there is this, sort of, purgatory that drags on requiring deeper and more meaningful thought. Some will prioritize money and make it their king. While others will realize there is little actual risk in business death to anything other than the ego. This is not to minimize the death, or even a blow, to the ego. These are painful internal wounds that are difficult to see. They require vulnerability to get any real healing, less another death is around the corner.

Business death requires self-surgery and real self-analyzation to revive your heart and awaken the God within or we will continue to give way to drifting and/or be enticed by awards and recognition away from our true purpose, just like Jesus in the desert.

In each moment I hope to be born better and new and to give myself the opportunity to be whole. Not just in business but in every moment. I keep very few awards or trophies. Most of them are stored in the garage until I throw them away a few years later, feeling guilty about tossing them out, but I am not these things.

Being removed from stuff gives me an opportunity to just live and die every day, to serve without guilt, to love, to speak my mind. I get to be wrong. I get to be right. I get to *live*. It is very freeing. Some people seek control and to be controlled, while others want to be free of control as it feels too great a burden to shoulder. Alan Watts, once again, gives us a pearl of wisdom and it starts and ends with *breath*.

> *"The curious thing about breath is that it can be looked at as both a voluntary and an involuntary action. You can feel on the one hand, I am doing it and on the other hand, it is happening to me. And that is why breathing is the most important part about meditation because it is going to show you, as you become aware of your breath, that the hard and fast division between what we do, on the one hand, and what happens to us on the other, is arbitrary.*
>
> *"So that as you watch your breathing you will become aware that both the voluntary and the involuntary aspects of your experience are all one happening.*
>
> *"Now that at first might seem a little scary because you may think well am I just the puppet of a happening, the mere passive witness of something that is happening beyond my control?*

> *Or on the other hand, am I really doing everything that is going along? If I were, I should be God and that would be very embarrassing because I would be in charge of everything. That would be a terribly responsible position.*
>
> *"The truth of the matter, as you will see it, is that both things are true. You can see that everything is happening to you, and the other hand you are doing everything." -Alan Watts*

If you say you are not God I will agree with you. You may not be there yet. You may still be asleep, a victim of your programming or circumstance, or I may be wrong entirely and we are all mere mortals scraping desperately for a meaning in this broken world before we take our exit.

Form your own opinions about God and it will help you see your business more clearly. I see God in every person I meet and choose to serve God in form; my precious children, my clients, my wife, myself, the stranger I pass in the streets. I *self-give* and avoid *self-sacrifice* because it puts a great burden on the person being sacrificed for and giving feels better anyway. Wouldn't you agree?

You may find your thoughts on God are not in line with your business and this may cause the feeling that *"there is no balance in my life"*. Of course there is no balance in your life! You think Church, work, family, and personal time are different things. They are all one in the same thing.

I have given you who I believe to be God; the person flipping through these pages, the person reading this on their tablet, or listening on audible, or the person who has never heard of *Zen Business*. You are God. All of you. If you aren't, you need to decide who you are and who you are not. Who are you? Why were you chosen? Who chose you? If you weren't chosen, why not you? What sort of God do you believe in? Is your God wrathful or forgiving? Controlling or loving? Warful or peaceful? I agree to all of it. Everything. You are quite right.

We spend far too much of life trying to derive meaning from it instead of giving it meaning through action. Can you truly derive a meaning from a story until you have finished it? Will the meaning be different for every character and every reader? If you were to ask me the meaning of my life I might say one thing but if I were to die tomorrow because I was struck by a drunk driver on the freeway someone might say that the meaning of that moment of my life was to not drink and drive, or worse that life is meaningless. They may be tempted, in their pain, to take away everything I was in this life or what it meant to me.

I will not concern myself too heavily with the meaning of life for it is constantly shifting and changing with every moment. Perhaps the meaning of life is to be present, or to love recklessly, or to be careful who you give your heart to, or to serve others, or to bring people

warm food, or to serve your community, or to become fully realized, or to go to heaven, or to help people realize they are enough. Let the spectators continue to decipher meaning. For them the meaning of life will have been to have quested for the meaning of life. How meaningless!
    Just live.
    Phew. You made it.
-le fou

Made in the USA
Columbia, SC
26 March 2021